INSIDE VERDICT:

A Changing Church in a Changing Scotland

Edited by Steve Mallon

Scottish
Christian PRESS

First published in Great Britain in 2003
by Scottish Christian Press
21 Young Street
Edinburgh
EH2 4HU

ISBN 1904325084

Design and layout by Heather Macpherson

Printed by Bookchase

Contents

Preface:

A WELCOME AND TIMELY DEBATE

Rev John C Christie
(Convener, Board of Parish Education)

It is a stimulating book; it attracted much attention, and encouraged significant and wide-ranging discussion. I refer, of course, to Harry Reid's *Outside Verdict*, with its sometimes devastating critique of the Church of Scotland. One of the strengths of that book is that it chimed with the times and has initiated a welcome and timely debate about what's wrong and what's right, with the Church of Scotland.

This book, for which I am privileged to write the Preface, is a contribution to that debate: but it is more than that, for it is designed to encourage the whole membership of the Church of Scotland in its faith journey. The reality is that the Church of Jesus Christ has always existed in a tension over what it should be, and what it is. Put simply, is our view of the Church inspired by the outlook that `the cup is half empty' or `the cup is half full'?

This book takes the latter view.

The present volume is not, however, simply a response to Harry Reid's book, but is born out of the many ideas that book raised, and the response many in the Church wanted to make to them. It sets the Church in the context of its time and place in early 21st century Scotland. It does more: it offers the reader an opportunity to face some of the key issues by looking at ourselves - as we are, and as we'd like to be; so that a newly conscious 'People of God' with renewing commitment may be able to live more confidently in the new millennium.

There is no doubt that the Church of Scotland is a changing church, though it can also be said that actually it's facing many of the same tensions of thought and theology which confronted the New Testament church - even to the casual reader of the New Testament it is very apparent that the Church never did have a Golden Age. So perhaps we shouldn't be too harsh on ourselves either. Maybe the Church's confidence is is to be found in a different way: by reflecting on the many opportunities its membership has continued to find to live faithfully the Gospel of Jesus Christ through such changing times. This is why we wanted to put this current book together: to highlight these and hearten ourselves by celebrating the transformation that a living faith in Jesus Christ can win.

Be transformed! Be encouraged!
I commend this book to you.
John C Christie

Introduction:

A CHANGING CHURCH IN A CHANGING SCOTLAND

Steve Mallon

The Church of Scotland today is many things and has many voices. Those who say it should only have one are missing the point of what the Church is supposed to be. One thing the Church of Scotland is not, is dying. It is alive. The numbers are certainly smaller, certainly, but that need not be the awful thing the doomsayers would have us believe. The challenges are indeed huge; but the Spirit of God is still at work and so we continue to reform ourselves and ask questions about where we go and what we do next: for example, the *Church without Walls* report and the subsequent discussions that have happened all over the country; and the efforts of the Assembly Council to reform the central structures of the Kirk; and the Task Force for Change which is a genuine attempt to radically alter ministry at the local level.

In 2002, a new book came out which specifically addressed the question of the Church of Scotland today: *Outside Verdict: An Old Kirk in a New Scotland*, written by Harry Reid; a *Glasgow Herald* journalist who was specifically asked to give the "outsider's" view of the Church. This was a significant event for the Church of Scotland and for a time it seemed like the whole country joined in a conversation about the future of the Church. The best thing about *Outside Verdict*, I think, is that it has got people talking about their church. That can only be a good thing - especially if it gives fresh impetus for reflection and change. Many people engaged with the book - well beyond the numbers who bought it. It was 'the talk o' the steamie' for a while. Hence this book - and *Inside Verdict* is not intended to be a critique of *Outside Verdict*: rather, it sets out to take up some of the major themes raised in that book. And there is an obvious need for another book like this: because as Harry Reid himself acknowledged, there is only so much that one man can do in one book. It seemed to us that there were obvious threads just waiting to be picked up at the end of *Outside Verdict*; and so the idea was born to write a book that would pick up and run with at least some of them. But this one is written by some committed insiders - people who are getting on with the job of changing the Kirk and dressing it in its new clothes for a new millennium.

Now, the Kirk today has two types of people. There are those who wring their hands, in a constant state of fear, and those who use their hands to get on with the job. This book is written by people who fit into the latter category. It's an interesting - perhaps strange - collection of people - people whom you wouldn't necessarily associate with each other: and yet here their voices speak together of hope for an institution that still has to run its God-given race. All of the contributors see the Kirk for what it is, and yet they choose to rejoice and to get on with the job. And the job is to build up the kingdom of God.

In the first section of the book, we look at some 'meta-themes': ideas and concepts that shape our lives together. How we view the church, our past and its future; how we view each other and issues that are difficult for us to face up to and deal with. This section opens with Peter Neilson making a plea for a new openness in the Kirk, an openness in our hearts and minds and a new openness to change. He does not operate from somewhere on cloud nine. He knows the Kirk and lists some of the key challenges ahead if we are to become a real church without walls. David Lacy and Marjory Maclean, perhaps as you would expect, then give an interesting account of the General Assembly. Their vision for this annual jamboree will either inspire you - or confirm your worst fears! But to see it through their eyes is to see the dangerous wonder of it. As the children in the Narnia books were always reminded, 'Aslan is not a tame lion'. Alison Twaddle then shows us her subversive side, encouraging us to deal with immoveable objects by circumnavigating them; and going on to make the point that in the old boy's network that is the church, many of its members are women! The church is run by women today - although led by men. Alison paints a warm picture in which the ministry of women can be appreciated afresh.

In 'Hearing the Evangelical Voice', Peter White has given us seven values to ponder: which, if followed, will give us a positive future and a more robust and authentically Christian experience at local and national levels. The Kirk has been accused at times of forgetting what it's there for: Peter reminds us of the point of our existence, and argues that perhaps now is a time to go back to first principles and rediscover the original idea for the church, before moving out in new directions. Following this, in 'The Last Taboo' Jane Denniston talks very openly and honestly about the Kirk's on-going struggle with sexuality. She does not offer comfort or clichés. There are voices to be heard in this chapter and they are not easy to hear. Will the issue of homosexuality split the Kirk? Jane discusses why that might happen, but also offers ways to avoid schism.

In the second and third sections we look at the Kirk on a more 'micro' level - with an emphasis on congregational life and ministry amongst adults, children and young people. This section opens with Iain Whyte giving us reasons to be cheerful. He suggests that in making an honest appraisal of ourselves there is much around to encourage us. There are still many of us. People are still interested in what we do. We can still achieve a lot with the energy we have. But the key problem he addresses is that of confidence. Has the church lost confidence; and if so, how can it rediscover it?

Susan Brown and Maureen Leitch give an interesting insight and vision to life in the local congregation. Susan Brown makes clear something that has been worrying her peers for a long time: what exactly is the role of the ordained clergy in this day and age? Maureen Leitch then makes a plea for a better conversation about congregational life, for us to see the possibilities that lie in every local body of Christ and for that body to be liberated to be all it can be.

Following the success of the *Year of the Child,* Doug Swanney is able to make a clear case for why the Kirk should listen to its children. He is a child of the Kirk himself and he has a big vision for the future of children's ministry because he sees so many signs of life. This is an area in which the church can claim to have some success stories which should inspire us onward.

Chris Docherty and I look at the issue of young people, from two perspectives. Chris Docherty paints an ecumenical picture; as an outsider who has had significant experiences within our walls and has some surprising things to say about who we are and what we look like. From the point of view of one who has been working with young people for a long time, I set out to track the recent history of the Kirk's relationship with young people and young adults, and suggest that something is happening of which we can be proud and which points to a brighter future than some might want to admit.

Back to back we then have Fiona Fidgin and Stewart Cutler, who also look at one issue from different perspectives. Fiona asks why so little emphasis is given to ministry among adults in the Church, while Stewart's piece shows clearly what happens when such ministry isn't available.

In the fourth section we consider how faith is flourishing amongst people and churches we might consider to be 'poor', and also celebrate the fact that in a day when we apparently live in a secular age the role of chaplaincy whether to schools, universities, hospitals or prisons seems to be gaining new ground - a ministry without walls perhaps?..

George Gammack starts this section, writing with deep passion about the many signs of life we see in congregations that we call 'UPA' or Urban Priority Area parishes. There is always a danger of writing off poor people and poor communities, and yet we must always remember that Jesus Christ was born in a stable - not in a palace. Written with a prophetic edge, perhaps the rebirth of the Church of Scotland is taking place in similarly humble surroundings?Then Alison Elliot discusses the growth in chaplaincy in a variety of institutions beyond the walls of the Kirk. For some these ministries represent a further drain on already scarce resources - mainly ordained clergy - and yet isn't there another way to look at this? If we believe in a Church without Walls, isn't this exactly the type of development we should be looking for?

And finally, the Moderator in what we might call the 'Year of Harry Reid', Very Rev John Miller wraps the whole project, considering the phenomenon of the Church as a whole - from perhaps a more informed overview than most, i.e. of a man put in the (impossible?) position of representing the whole spectacle - as the visible "Head" of the Church. If we, and Harry Reid, found it difficult to present a fair picture of the Church as a whole (and the editor would like honestly to admit here, that - having set out to 'redress the balance' - we did!) - what portion of it can one person in one year hope to address? John gives us his answer.

So there you have it. A cornucopia of ideas, passion, despair, hope, fears, expectations and honesty. These are not "company men", and women. They are the movers and shakers, in that they are the people who have raised their heads above the parapets and have seen the new land. They are like the ancients who were sent to explore the land promised to the Israelites:

> They came back to Moses and Aaron and the whole Israelite community at Kadesh in the Desert of Paran. There they reported to them and to the whole assembly and showed them the fruit of the land. They gave Moses this account: 'We went into the land to which you sent us, and it does flow with milk and honey! Here is its fruit. But the people who live there are powerful, and the cities are fortified and very large. We even saw descendants of Anak there. The Amalekites live in the Negev; the Hittites, Jebusites and Amorites live in the hill country; and the Canaanites live near the sea and along the Jordan.'
>
> Then Caleb silenced the people before Moses and said, 'We should go up and take possession of the land, for we can certainly do it.' But the men who had gone up with him said, 'We can't attack those people; they are stronger than we are.' And they spread among the Israelites a bad report about the land they had explored. They said, 'The land we explored devours those living in it. All the people we saw there are of great size. We saw the Nephilim there (the descendants of Anak come from the Nephilim). We seemed like grasshoppers in our own eyes, and we looked the same to them.'
>
> (Numbers 13:27-33)

We know the rest of the story. Perhaps this time the people of God will accept that in the new land there will be challenges and difficulties, but that we will go there anyway. The promised land exists. We have wandered in the desert long enough. It's time to move on. The people in this book have a sense of wonder about that new place and reckon we can do it. So, shall we?

Steve Mallon
May 2003

Section 1:

The State of the Union: A look at the overall picture

One:

AN OPEN DOOR - IN A *CHURCH WITHOUT WALLS*

Peter Neilson

Rev Peter Neilson has been Associate Minister at the Parish Church of St Cuthbert since 1997. Prior to that he was minister in Mount Florida in Glasgow (1975-86) ,and then Adviser in Mission and Evangelism with the Board of National Mission, including five years at St Ninian's, Crieff. He was Convener of the Special Commission which produced the "Church without Walls" report in 2001. From the summer of 2003, he is to be Mission Developments Facilitator, supporting the work of churches under the New Charge Committee of the Board of National Mission.

'It opens doors for people.'[1] That was the succinct inside verdict of the Very Rev Andrew McLellan on the *Church without Walls* report in 2001 . Without worrying about the obvious pun, that imagery would be a satisfying verdict for the people who produced it. A couple of years on, the prophetic comment stands true.

From the outset, there was an air of excitement and possibility. For the Commissioners at the 2001 Assembly, the *Church without Walls* report put into words what many people were working towards in their churches. One minister who would consider himself radical complained that it made him look mainstream! He laughed and said he would have to move further to the edge. For others it gave voice to a vision they already cherished. Now they had more confidence to go for it! This was not seen as an official report from "above". It came from "within", articulating a vision that the Spirit had already written on their hearts.

That is the first, and most significant, open door - an open door to the hearts and minds of many elders and ministers who pray for the renewal of the Church in our land.

The second open door is less obvious, but no less significant. Among the decision-makers around the Church there seems to be a new openness to change. Those who hold positions of power seem to be willing to consent and become midwives of the emerging church, rather than defenders of the status quo.

When the aspirations of the grass-roots chime with the hopes of the decision-makers, then unexpected doors swing open for new dreams to be fulfilled. That does not mean

---

[1] Report of the Special Commission Anent Review and Reform; *Reports to the General Assembly of the Church of Scotland 2001*, reprinted as *Church without Walls*, Parish Education Publications 2001.

that turning dreams into reality is easy. But it does create a new climate of hope and a culture of possibility.

Follow me

'Follow me'. That simple but inexhaustible call of Jesus lies at the heart of *Church without Walls*. The Church is described from the Gospels as 'people with Jesus at the centre, travelling where Jesus takes them.'[2]

People have responded to that direct focus on Jesus Christ and the call to discipleship. Congregations have chosen to 'live with a Gospel for a year'[3]. Booklets have been produced. Sermons have been preached. Groups have met. Lives have been changed. One rural congregation invited people to meet monthly to consider the practical implications of the Gospel passages they had been studying. Another city congregation encouraged reflective worship on Gospel passages. What difference would it make to our lives personally and corporately if we let some of these stories of Jesus shape our behaviour?

Church life has become overly complicated. People have welcomed the simplicity of that focus on Christ as recommended in the CWW report. The paradox is that simplicity leads us to new depths with God. Much of our congregational organisation creates sophisticated hiding-places from a living encounter with Christ. We lament the lack of resources for many of our schemes, but a former Dean of St Paul's Cathedral suggested all we need is 'memory, vision - and a little bread and wine would help.' *Church without Walls* is a call to be a simpler church.

Community connections

Church without Walls conjures up images of connections with the community. Some rural parishes have responded indignantly that church and community overlap already. Other churches recognise how disconnected they have become from the life of the community and have taken up the challenge of a community audit. This may be necessary because the changes in our communities are more rapid and more subtle than we realise.

It has been suggested that we could cure our isolationism by living the agenda of Matthew 25 - shaping our life to be the church of the stranger, the sick, the prisoner or the hungry. That way we put Christ at the centre in the person of 'one of the least of these', and travel to be where Jesus takes us. We could tour the country and find examples of that kind of caring - day care for elderly folks with dementia, a side chapel with a tree of remembrance and memorial books for bereaved families, international exchanges to see Africa or India face to face. People who have never read the report

2 *Church without Walls,*. p 9
3 *Church without Walls,* p. 18

speak of doing things 'in the spirit of *Church without Walls*' - which is obviously a great encouragement. There are as many open doors to the community as there are people to be served.

Friends together

One critique of the *Church without Walls* report claimed that it said little about being a community. The writer went on to advocate that we learn from people like Jean Vanier to be a therapeutic community, or from Stanley Hauerwas to be 'communities of character'. While the word community does not appear often in the language of the report, its fundamental thrust is to call the church to a 'relational reformation' expressing the grace of Christ in all our relationships. Most significantly, the idea behind CWW puts the power of community-building into the hands of ordinary people by encouraging us to be friends.

It was C S Lewis who spoke of two motifs for Christian community. He warned against the motif of lovers, where people are captivated by each other to the exclusion of others. He encouraged us rather to be as friends, who stand shoulder to shoulder to face a common task or a common journey.[4]

It is well known that people are attracted to the Christian faith through significant relationships. The loss of young people from our churches can often result from the cold shoulder of established members who treat them as strangers rather than friends. Creative youth work can be found all around Scotland, and there are good examples in youth-related chapters in this book. Many young people go on to be disciples of Christ, where the generation gap is overcome by a relational bridge that welcomes and affirms them as part of the worshipping and serving community of faith. For instance, the success of *Alpha* courses across the world is due to the quality of genuine friendships as searchers find fellow-travellers on the way. As the walls come down between denominations, too, there are more and more examples of ecumenical partnerships in worship and mission in our towns and cities.

There was some disappointment among congregations in Urban Priority Areas that the *Church without Walls* report - and the General Assembly response to it - did not deliver more money to areas of need, or challenge some of the structural barriers that mask the face of Christ from the poorest in our land. Nonetheless, there was a strong call for churches in different social contexts to establish mutual partnerships. As the Urban Priority Area voices are heard more clearly through the recent report on *Sharing the Pain - Holding the Hope*[5], that call will be more clearly focused to encourage the fifty most wealthy congregations to link up with the fifty poorest. If that door of relationship can be opened, then many other good things will flow both ways through the opening.

[4] Lewis, CS, *The Four Loves*, Geoffrey Bles Ltd, Harper Collins, 1960 p 79
[5] Report of the Board of National Mission: *Reports to the General Assembly of the Church of Scotland 2002*, pp 20/13-26

Gifts galore!

Perhaps the part of the *Church without Walls* report which attracts most approval is the call to recognise and release the gifts of all God's people in worship and witness. Kirk Sessions are being revamped so that people can serve God in line with their passion and God-given talent. There are congregations where the concern to offer quality bereavement care has led to elders being equipped to conduct funerals. This is not about diminishing the role of the Ordained Minister or simply about a pragmatic response to ministerial shortages. Instead it is about discovering anew what it means to be the Body of Christ in our day. Where finances are available, churches are employing staff teams as administrators, secretaries, youth workers, pastoral assistants and other roles. Much of the focus of this development lies in administration, pastoral care, mission and contributing to the leading of worship. In other words their gifts are expressed in the church when it is gathered or organised as the visible church presence in the community.

However, increasing attention is also being given to affirming Christians in their place of work. This is the primary place of Christian service for most people from Monday to Saturday - in shops, schools, farms, businesses, hospitals, factories or hotels. Many are struggling with the 'double isolation' of being the only Christian at work, or feeling that church is an extra burden rather than a support for living.

Here is the *Church without Walls* idea expressed without even trying! Saturday morning 'bacon roll groups', intercessions led by people from different walks of life, lunchtime discussions during the working week based around faith and work - all these and more are ways of recognising the gifts of people as they go about being the church day by day.

They think it's all over...

Of course, there are people who have not even started on this journey of discovery. That is fine. We are playing a long game. *Church without Walls* will likely continue to open doors for a long time to come. Some people see the influence coming in waves. At the moment we are in the first phase of local engagement. A number of Church Boards are shaping their work and policy on the principles of the report. For instance, the Board of National Mission and the Board of Parish Education have shaped elements of their work to match the themes of the report, and the General Trustees have reviewed, in the light of emerging patterns of ministry, a more flexible use of the substantial funds which they hold in trust. A few Presbyteries are working at it. The Presbytery of Irvine and Kilmarnock has created a strategy to encourage all congregations to study and implement the report, while the Presbytery of Perth is meeting congregations to develop a 'regional needs plan' for training. In Orkney, the Community Minister has developed a scheme to create worship teams in congregations. There are signs that some small neighbouring Presbyteries are looking at creative patterns of cooperation and others are re-examining their style of meeting and administration. By 2005 there will be nation-wide celebrations that will be designed to encourage us to see the emerging profile of the *Church without Walls*, and to discern the next step of obedience to God's calling.

With the stirrings of any new movement there will be those who stand on the sidelines and view it with cynicism or even belligerent disapproval. However, with around one-third of the congregations of the Church of Scotland actively engaged with the themes of the Report, and many others working in tune with its ethos, there are signs of a church being reshaped by the Spirit to share in God's mission in our generation.

The Boards of Parish Education, Stewardship and National Mission have been enthusiastically offering people and resources to help churches move forward. The themes of *Church without Walls* have been digested by the consultants and advisers, who work with congregations. They offer booklets, videos and, most of all, personal support for churches who are ready to make this journey. The Board of World Mission has entered into conversation with our worldwide partners to hear from them on evangelism, theological education, lay training, sharing resources and mission in our pluralistic context. When we learn of 700 lay people being trained in Jamaica, we are reminded of the untapped potential of our churches where ministers are assumed to do it all. The Presbyterian Church of Singapore offers a 39-week course on discipleship for all members, with 3-4 hours teaching each week. It has been humbling to hear that our partners were honoured to be asked to advise mother church in Scotland! One African partner commented that the Church of Scotland 'looks like a church that has gone to bed'! If we have ears to hear, let us hear!

In these days of international travel, the local church can and should be a global church. In the world of the internet, local no longer means parochial. The doors are open to the world.

Church without Walls has influenced three other fundamental areas of church life - the area of spirituality, team ministry and financial priorities.

Spirituality today

Spirituality has entered the language of our culture, replacing the defensive language of religion and religious affiliation. There have been explorations of old strands of Christian spirituality - Ignatian, Celtic, Reformed and Benedictine, to name only a few. We hear of spirituality in the world of business and management. In Douai Abbey near

Reading, a Benedictine order offers "executive retreats" to help the leaders of business to recover balance in life. In the world of health care, the Scottish Executive is sponsoring research into spirituality within the healthcare service. Research from Nottingham University reminds us that people outside the church are 60% more likely to speak of spiritual experiences today than they would in 1987, when the last research was done.[6]

Churches are offering people space for spiritual exploration in reflective worship, retreats in life, or exploring the spirituality of women and/or men. In the various churches people are rediscovering the mysterious power of walking the ancient labyrinth of Chartres as a way of coming close to God and then returning to life in God's world. *Church without Walls* invited people to lay down paths for the spiritual journey so that we take a fresh look at following Jesus Christ in our post-modern times. Paths are being formed by people walking them.

Teamwork

The call for team ministry is relatively straightforward to implement within a parish, if we are determined to disciple people and train leaders according to their gifts and callings. There are excellent examples of sustained and thorough team-building in various churches across the land. The trouble comes when we want to create teams that will cross over inherited parish boundaries, and to place a multi-disciplinary team in that enlarged area to serve it. Suddenly we are up against questions of the congregation's right to call a minister, and the minister's right to 'tenure'.

Already, there are pilot schemes where three or four parishes have been brought together: though not into a union, in the old sense of one or two ministers for them all. Now a team leader is appointed; a pastoral worker is recruited; a youth worker or deacon may follow. Local volunteers are to be recruited and trained for specific tasks according to the needs of the area.

Within the Church of Scotland a 'task force for change' is addressing all the knotty problems of call, tenure, buildings and necessary support to make the transitions. These are the practical and troubling aspects of creating a *Church without Walls*. Old certainties have to make way for a new culture of flexibility. But it is happening!

Money, money, money

Money is still God's chief rival. We either serve one or the other. It is hardly surprising that the tough battles come when we reshape the Church to a new agenda and have to move the resources to fund the vision.

[6] Hay, David and Hunt, Kay, *Understanding the Spirituality of People who don't go to Church: A report on the findings of the Adults' Spirituality Project*, University of Nottingham, p 12

The *Church without Walls* report tackled this at two levels. The first was to call for a Parish Development Fund, which would make significant funds available to fuel local visionary projects. That fund has been set up with a Project Worker and a starting fund of £3 million over the next five years. Too many dreams never become reality because churches have to cajole fund-giving bodies around the country. How much better that they should be able to approach mother church for significant support.

The larger issue of finance lies in the concern that there was no process for determining financial priorities within the Church of Scotland as a whole. *Church without Walls* indicated that as an urgent task to be tackled through the Coordinating Forum, under the guidance of the Assembly Council. The Coordinating Forum comprises the Conveners and Secretaries of Boards and Committees, and meets to confer on changes in their own internal budgets. Everyone was agreed that new processes were needed to look at agreeing overall priorities, but the mechanism has been a long slow series of consultations.

The process is far from complete, but there are signs of a new spirit abroad. Despite all the inevitable struggles about defending budgets and work that each Department of the Church deems vital, there have been very far-reaching conversations which will allow the Church to realign its finances to the emerging priorities of our mission in the 21st century. In a real sense the walls are coming down as various sections of the church learn to work together for the common good of the Gospel in Scotland and beyond.

One of the decisions by the authors of *Church without Walls* was to avoid the cynicism which sometimes colours discussions about '121 George Street' and outlying departments - the central administration of the Church of Scotland. That kind of scape-goating achieves nothing. There are still walls to come down and doors to open, but the Church at the centre is changing.

Beyond *Church without Walls*

However, it would not be in the spirit of *Church without Walls* to end with talk about money and structures. They should be the servants of the Kingdom, never controllers of the agenda. *Church without Walls* was never meant to be the last word on the shape of the church. Already there are new shoots of the church emerging across the land that are very unlike anything we have seen. In our Urban Priority Areas, the church is operating in the slipstream of the coming Kingdom of God. God is among the poor of our society and there is a radical call coming to the Church to ensure that Christ's church is nurtured and sustained in these places of great need and great opportunity.

For the first time in forty years, we are planting new churches in areas of new development or where the Church has become too weak to rise again to the challenge.

New charges are being formed in greenfield and brownfield sites across Scotland. There are areas of decline and death, but the God of Resurrection is raising up new churches for a new generation. Churches such as Oldmachar in Aberdeen, Riverside in Perth or Whiteinch in Glasgow are shaped by the determination to be authentic missional communities. Where the inherited pattern of church is too rigid to engage with this culture, seeds of new churches are being sown where the lead line is to connect with the new generation who make little sense of most church life today. A bold step to develop a "church for a new generation" is recently underway in Gilmerton in South East Edinburgh, supported by the prayers and goodwill of the neighbouring parishes.

In a society that is often more at home in networks than in neighbourhoods, we are seeing 'network' churches being formed in areas of business and leisure. One city centre church has developed a 'church without walls' in the local business community, and is exploring the church for the clubbing cultures of the city. These network churches will become the ways in which many people find Christ and are equipped to serve Christ in their everyday lives. People with Jesus at the centre will travel where Jesus takes them. We are being transformed from the 'solid state' church into 'liquid church', finding our way into every nook and cranny of society.

Some of us have had a good innings in the Church as we know it, but find the notion of change is uncomfortable. Spare a thought for the grandchildren who are now two generations away from Church. Hard as it is for us to admit, the Church-for-us has often been in the way of these younger ones finding Christ. We know that they need to know Christ as much as we need him. We either stand in the way of the changes that will make that possible, or we give consent to a new church for a new culture.

In Psalm 84, the Psalmist talks of being a 'doorkeeper in the house of the Lord'. If there is to be an open door for the missing generations of Scotland, we need people to hold that door open for them so that they can invent a church for their own time.

We need doorkeepers in a *Church without Walls*! Somebody out there is looking for an open door!

Two

THE 850 HIGH HEID YINS OF THE CHURCH: CURRENT REFORMING TRENDS IN THE GENERAL ASSEMBLY

David W Lacy and Marjory A MacLean

Rev David W Lacy is Convener of the Board of Practice and Procedure, and of the Business Committee, of the Assembly. He is minister of Henderson Church, Kilmarnock, an enthusiastic sailor and a keen singer. His colleagues regard him as a gentle sorter-outer of situations and people, in the nicest possible way. **Rev Marjory A MacLean** is Depute Clerk to the Assembly and has acted as Clerk of the Assemblies of 2002 and 2003. A former parish minister, and, like David, keen on choral singing, Marjory has been described as everything from 'fierce' to 'fluffy', rather depending on whom you ask.

The visitor to the Oxbridge Quad admired the weedless perfection of its lawns and asked the Master how it was achieved and flawlessly maintained. 'Roll the ground, plant it with grass… and mow it every day for 400 years,' came the reply.

This is an essay about the General Assembly, written by two people who share some of the responsibility for its future, and who constantly face the question whether to keep mowing to keep the Assembly unchangingly pristine, or whether to take a great big yellow digger to it and plant something different altogether. We believe that recent critics of the General Assembly have not been nearly drastic enough in the reforms they have suggested; they have succumbed to the temptation to focus on the form and process of the General Assembly, when all the time the content of its business is an untapped possibility of dramatic debate and memorable affirmations. An endless rumbling critique of the colourful wrapping of our biggest annual event fails to call the whole Church to open its mouth and be exciting.

The paragraphs that follow look at the things the Assembly is there to do, and the things it is good at doing. We intend to share, in each case, the things that make us clench our fists and say 'yes!', the things that make the third Saturday of May one of our favourite days of the year.

What does the whole Church need to do? - the Assembly as legislature

The Assembly is a legislative body that represents the spiritual leadership of the Church, whose members vote according to personal study, consideration and conscience on the basis of the arguments they have heard and the materials they have read. No-one going to the General Assembly has to decide in advance what his or her position is on any topic, nor compile a manifesto, nor subscribe to a political programme to secure a seat, nor join a theological party and be subject to its whip. No member of the General Assembly has to set aside what seems right to do what seems popular: each one is dangerously free and each one has a constituency no smaller than the whole Church.

In exchange for their direct and undirected power, these 850 (the only 'high heid yins' the Church possesses) owe a huge responsibility to ensure that they do represent the needs of those who might have constituted an electorate in a different system. In a Christian organisation, however, it is not good enough just to represent the majority opinion of a constituency: the responsibility and the thrill of the job is to be risky and dangerous, to say upsetting things about the world in the Assembly (where they will make a difference and cause a splash), and to say new alarming things to the thousands scattered around the Church who prefer to keep things as they are because it will 'see them out'. It is the responsibility to do for the wider Church the things you might not even think of doing in your own wee corner: your own wee corner may not happen to need this measure; but at the other end of the country, the need may be desperate. It is the responsibility to be a whole Church, and to put into practical effect the love and prayers we offer to others. It is the responsibility to think that what is good enough for Dumfries is good enough for Lerwick, and what is the minimum acceptable standard for Barnton should be the minimum acceptable standard for Possilpark.

You can change Assembly procedure until you are blue in the face: but it is the content put into those procedures that will change the Church and the world.

What is the Church up to? - the Assembly as executive accountability

Presbyterianism as "institutionalised distrust"[1] is a fear and a threat, and many of the suggestions contained in this essay are pleas for greater trust in the competence and motivation of those who can be left to get on with things without any court breathing constantly down their necks.

To some extent, however, the limits of trust are the very foundation of Presbyterian Church management. Every day, and in every action, our paid and unpaid servants have immediate access to the places where they are held accountable in the lower courts and the central boards and committees: there the work is analysed, and detailed decisions of micro-policy made. In the third week of May, the committees report their

---

[1] *Church without Walls*, Parish Education Publications 2001 p 16

diligence, accept the wider scrutiny of the whole Church and receive the big changes of direction and strategy - the macro-policy - that become their new brief and fresh remit.

The sport of 121-bashing is a different, and less helpful, thing altogether. Pretending that officials are accountable only to the General Assembly - and therefore only in one week out of every fifty-two - is sheer mischief, ignoring the constant, watching brief of the committees: changing tack to impugn the integrity of those committees takes the philosophy of distrust to a silly extent. (You do not, for example, stop living in a parliamentary democracy just because the House of Commons happens to be in recess this week.) Moreover, being accountable means, for employees in the Church Offices, being protected; so it's not something they would sensibly try to avoid!

But how wide does that accountability have to be? How many Presbyterians *does* it take to change a light-bulb? Who knows what the optimum size of the General Assembly may turn out to be? The authors both believe there is one criterion that mustn't be lost in that debate: that in a Presbyterian Church, power and authority belong to all the ministers, deacons and elders, be it locally, regionally or nationally, and so the General Assembly should not shrink so much that the authority appears to be located in individual persons. The tiny, flexible Assembly, characterised by consultative exercises - the dream of some - would lose the essential strength of a Church where the *whole* spiritual leadership rules over the whole bureaucratic management.

The scope for radical reform lies in that balance of trust. A Church confident enough in its best leaders and managers can remit tasks to individuals, and the supervision of those tasks to very tiny groups. Such a Church (for instance the Uniting Church of Australia tries to live like this) can remove management from the business of its courts and free Assemblies, Presbyteries and Kirk Sessions for the infinitely more exciting task of leadership.

We hope that one year soon a big Board will bring to our Assembly a report that begins like this: 'We have continued to fulfil the whole remit contained in our constitution, and have implemented the laws of the Church and all the instructions to us and affirmations of recent General Assemblies. The remainder of this brief report outlines suggestions for new theological affirmations and fresh remits for the leading edge of our department's work.' If the General Assembly of that year has the grace of trust, it will receive the report with warm approval and questions expressive of interest rather than criticism, and spend most of the two hours allocated to that debate wrestling over the big issues of principle and future strategy. That's our dream: that's the change the Assembly needs more than anything.

What on earth has the Church done? - the Assembly as judicial power

No part of the Assembly's job has been more reformed in recent decades than its task of weeding out the Church's daftest decisions, and righting the wrongs done in other places.

To the Commission of Assembly and the Judicial Commission have long since been passed those reviews that concern decisions of detail on technical matters, or the implementation of set policies. Those bodies share that problem of optimum size, requiring to be large enough to represent the interests of the Church but small enough to grapple with matters of detail and complexity and bulk and sensitivity. The Church *semper reformanda* will agonise over those questions in all time coming, but they do not belong to this essay.

To the General Assembly itself is left the big, dramatic approaches, the issues of doctrine and widest strategy, the moments when the whole Church is called to account from outside itself. To the General Assembly itself comes the individual petitioner - not even necessarily a member of the Church - who has exhausted every other avenue to disentangle their problem. To the General Assembly comes the lower court that has had a flash of inspiration about a point of principle and wants to make a suggestion for everyone to hear.

That avenue of approach is a deeply dangerous aperture in the General Assembly, a deliberate point of vulnerability with the potential for terrible consequences. It is an aperture through which terrible mistakes can be made, when the power of passionate rhetoric has the force to lead the court to think with its heart and not its head. It is also an aperture through which the Holy Spirit can be unleashed, when - again! - the power of passionate rhetoric has the force to lead the court to think with its heart and not its head. So we could not be prouder of the danger of it. It is the part of the Assembly over which the managers have least control, and where the leaders of the moment are hardest to identify in advance.

Whose we are and Whom we serve - the Assembly as worshipping community

For a long time Assembly worship has been an easy target for some - although those who describe it as old-fashioned should bear in mind that it now uses more technological devices and modern praise resources than many congregations do. (Although we did resist the not-entirely-serious suggestion of a former Procurator, that the words of the Psalms be displayed on the big screens with the aid of a bouncy-ball, karaoke-style.) Those unaccompanied psalms that attract particular criticism from determined modernists are in fact a favourite element of too many Assembly-goers, including youth representatives, to be a safe target. In readings and homilies, the Assembly forms a learning community as well as being a celebrating one throughout the week, so there is no shortage of seriousness for those who seek it.

The contemporary Church, fulfilling her ministry in many ways more than through its traditional parish Churches, is learning to worship in vast numbers and tiny handfuls, in the pauses of a working day and in huge special events away from consecrated buildings. Less and less does the worship of everyday conform to a comfortable, recognisable pattern, and more and more do people develop acts of worship that are unique events. The General Assembly is one place for doing things that cannot be done anywhere else, when it is over-run by a children's choir from Africa, or led in prayer by members of our own Children's Forums, or hearing a Bible reading by a mission partner at the end of a very, very long telephone line.

Long may the worship of the Assembly be the favourite bit for some people, and raise the eyebrows of others.

Does anyone notice? - Church-State symbolism

The General Assembly of a Church without walls needs to be something certain people cannot help but notice. A national Church ministers not only to isolated individuals but to people in communities; so it needs to have a relationship with corporate bodies, councils, parliaments and all the people who facilitate the celebration of community throughout the country. Those community leaders, as often as not, willingly acknowledge the work and worth of the Church and make connections of goodwill, if not of commitment, towards our work.

The Assembly might arguably cope without the Monarch's High Commissioner, but would be the poorer for lack of a host for others who are there for just the same reason. The politicians and lawyers, soldiers and councillors, and all the other bits and pieces of social glue that form the Assembly's outer ring, provide the hearing ear of a wider society, waiting for us in the Assembly to say amazing, shocking things to them.

Your attitude to those little pieces of ceremony is founded by how you see the first moment of each Assembly day. A member of what Andrew Marr calls 'the anti-Establishment establishment' will see the Assembly bowing to the High Commissioner as some kind of monarchist gesture, and him condescendingly returning the bow. But the closer watcher with the open mind will notice that no-one moves a neck-muscle until the High Commissioner has begun his bow, for he is paying the respects of the society he represents to the court he is visiting, and the General Assembly does nothing more than acknowledge his respects by returning his gesture.

We look for nothing more than what we receive, that the world's leadership stops for a moment and takes the trouble to say 'Church of Scotland, we see you there and we acknowledge what you're trying to do and say'.

Daring to enjoy it - the Assembly as a social event

Two first-time commissioners bravely set off from different B+B establishments the night before the 2002 Assembly began, to attend the briefing social laid on for them. Back home, they had done all the reading they could, asked all the questions they dared to, watched the introductory video for Commissioners[2] - known to all those who've seen it as 'the fish-and-chips video' - and hoped like mad that someone would fill in the gaps in their knowledge and give them a sense of what to expect. Certainly each felt rather alone and a little nervous. A glass of wine and a couple of hours later, the pair of them accepted a lift from an Assembly official back to their guest houses, which turned out to be in the same road, and made an arrangement to travel and sit together at the opening session the next morning.

Church people can be cursed with the false sense of having fears that are unique - fears of leading worship for the first time, or surviving a vacancy, or taking on the eldership, or trying to sort out a dispute inside the congregation. The General Assembly's magic is its ability to build a community that is almost instantly strong, relying on the warmth of those who have a special responsibility for helping others, and being blessed by the good nature of so many others, too. In that welcoming atmosphere, new members of the Assembly realise that they are not alone, and the reasons for their nervousness turn out to have friendly faces - and a few nerves of their own!

Our odd recipe for radical reform of the General Assembly includes the plea to take terribly seriously the social side of it. Commissioners who attend from Monday to Thursday, rushing off mid-afternoon to get the train back to their parish and accepting no invitations to anything, will most certainly find the Assembly a poor thing and rather short on inspiration. For not even when radical debate has one day swept away dreary management-reports will the Assembly really change its members' outlooks, not unless its members get in amongst the social mortar that sticks together the bricks of business, meeting real people from different places, different traditions, even different churches, to hear their stories in the drawing room of a palace or in the conversation at a reception or over a pie in a pub.

Whose business is it anyway? - the Assembly as a consultative exercise

Lots of people stick their fingers, or at least their wisdom, into the business of the Assembly. Delegates from other churches in Britain and throughout the world, along with Youth Representatives (sent by Presbyteries and from the National Youth Assembly) regularly use the power of a fresh perspective or someone else's experience to stop our Church from re-inventing a wobbly wheel, or failing to notice the call of God from an

[2] So You're Going to Be a Commissioner, Board of Practice and Procedure, 2002

unlikely angle, or shaping our Church only for our own generation. The occasional invasion by children - something it is hoped to develop over a regular cycle of involvement in the life of the national Church as a response to the recent Year of the Child - does no harm in waking up some sleepy-heads.

These are the groups who give the Assembly its festive atmosphere, who add colours and accents and desires which it is a challenge to hear and address. Free of the responsibility of decision-making, they are able to throw their spanners into the worst of our works and rock boats at will. The Church need be diverted by only a degree or two from its previous course for it to arrive at a refreshingly different destination; sometimes such a nudge is exactly what we need, and we try to make it easy for them to make it difficult for us.

As long as the business of the General Assembly is about management of institutions and not discernment of policy, little will be gained from extending consultation, or group-work, or conference-style debating of issues: the amount of business to be got through just does not give time for these more reflective and informal styles, as members of badly-run Kirk Sessions in large congregations can testify. It also loses once again the whole point of having the committees of the Church, where consultation can meet knowledge and professional solutions can be developed for specialist situations. In the General Assembly, the only thing we should expect each member to be knowledgeable about is being a disciple of Jesus Christ: the expertise emerges from the fascinating combination of people who make up the Assembly in its plenary debates, and the place for individual consultation is, perhaps most effectively, in the committee rooms during the other 51 weeks of each year.

Abuse of the system - a positive plea

In short, we think that if the General Assembly could celebrate its trust in the Presence of God for which it prays each morning - if it could trust its own employees, Boards and Committees, ceding much of its management role to them - then this annual event could serve all sorts of revival in the church's life. If people commissioned and called to lead God's people could be given some air there, the Assembly could have the capacity to make society nervous - with big debates on small reports, rhetoric bouncing between the walls of the Assembly Hall, and a puzzled, bemused, interested people of Scotland.....certain that we are up to something!

Three:

BEYOND THE OLD BOYS' NETWORK

Alison Twaddle

Alison Twaddle is currently General Secretary of the Church of Scotland Guild; formerly, she was Europe Secretary in the Department of World Mission. She is a member of the congregation of Belhaven, East Lothian, where she serves as a leader in the children's learning programme, Launchpad. She is also a member of the Guild there and takes part in various worship and study groups. Following an earlier period of freelance work as a translator of books for an international publishing company, she has also contributed to several reference works for that publisher, most enjoyably their Dictionary of Literary Characters.

Why can't a woman be more like a man?

Two cartoons hang on my office wall. The first, an old *Punch* cartoon, shows several men and one woman seated round a Boardroom table. The chairman is saying, *'That's an excellent idea, Miss Triggs. Perhaps one of the men would like to suggest it'*. The second, by Larry, shows a businessman arriving home to a scene of devastation in the family kitchen. The note on the table reads: *'Gone berserk, your dinner's on the ceiling.'*

It's a neat summary of the contemporary female dilemma. Be a corporate woman and be patronised beyond endurance, or take up the domestic role and be driven to extreme measures in order to gain any recognition at all. Of course both are exaggerations of the reality; that's what makes them work as humour. But there's enough truth in there to make them worth a second look some days. What strikes me, as I look at them now, is the complete bafflement on the faces of the men in the pictures. They just don't get it. They are the visual equivalent of the bemused voice of Richard Harris singing 'How to handle a woman' in the film version of *Camelot*, or the exasperation of Rex Harrison's Higgins in *My Fair Lady*, asking: 'Why can't a woman be more like a man?'

Everything would just be fine, these poor guys feel, if only the women would play by the club rules. No disrespect to the ladies you understand, they've got a lot to offer; they just have to learn how to fit in.

In the church, as in many large, long-established organisations, the old boys' network still retains some influence, though thankfully that is being challenged. It's worth pointing out too, that often it's more a question of attitude than of gender; some of the old boys are female and some of those who challenge - or increasingly ignore - its power, are male. The trouble with any old boy network is its capacity to stymie anything it has neither generated nor owned; the Miss Triggs syndrome in other words. An idea may seem quite sound, exciting even, but if it comes from someone who is not "one of us", can we really be sure it will fly? Better be cautious, better add a disclaimer, send it down to presbyteries, set up a working group.

This is to do with the 'alphas' (usually male) in any group; those who emerge and function as the pack leaders. In human corporate terms the alphas aren't necessarily the ones with the best decision-making skills or most original ideas; they are simply the ones who look and behave as if they have the right to the authority they exercise. The more they are deferred to, the harder it is to challenge their power. But someone, sometime, has to, and it's amazing how hard that can be. I confess that, at one time, there were occasions when I would wear a grey trouser suit in order to make it easier for the alpha males to recognise, by my plumage, that I too had a voice and opinions to offer and - scariest of all for the old boys in the network - *questions* to ask. For a definition of defensive, you can't do better than a committee of the church that has been asked a telling question.

There is, however, more than one way to deal with an immoveable object. Where force proves all too resistible, circumnavigation can be a rewarding alternative. In other words, go round the obstacle, like a fast-flowing stream round a boulder in its path. This is what is happening in refreshing ways in the life of the church. It's a mark of life to resist arbitrary confinement and there *is* life out there, beyond the old boys' network.

Recognising wisdom where she may be found

I reckon I have had opportunities to see, more than most, the rich variety of local church life. As General Secretary of the Church of Scotland Guild (and the Guild is most definitely not "one of us"), I've covered a lot of miles to meet, and speak to, the members of the Guild and the Church; and it has been an experience at times frustrating and depressing, but also often startling and inspiring. Sure, I've been to meetings that were hard going: the draughty church hall, the unimaginative worship, the unresponsive audience. But I don't honestly think I've ever been to a single one where there hasn't been something to leaven that lump, be it the sharing of a sorrow in the very last moment of the evening as someone sees me to my car, the discovery of an unexpected link in the small world of Scottish church life, or the cup of tea I will never disparage, having once memorably learned that this was indeed an offering of a talent, a ministry.

And I've been to other meetings when I've wanted to say 'thank you' for the privilege of letting me share in something profoundly moving, or intellectually challenging. I went once to a small afternoon Guild in the central belt, specifically invited to lead a meeting on the 2001-2 Discussion Topic, 'Overcoming Violence'. No-one had felt up to this challenge and so I agreed to go along and show them how. What arrogance, as I was to discover. No, they didn't feel comfortable with breaking into groups; could I not just talk about the subject? Of course I could - talking's what I'm really good at. My first impression of the group was that they were my mother's age group, educated at a time when pupils were not encouraged to speak freely in class, when learning happened by listening and remembering what had been said. Then I reckoned they must have lived through the Second World War and I asked them what they could remember about the outbreak of war and what it had meant for them. That was enough from me. For the rest of that memorable session, I listened and I learned. The bitter fruit of violence was something they knew, up close and personal. Sometimes I can't help feeling that all this experience is going to waste in the church - that too few people recognise that there might be a valuable contribution to be made from this section of the church family. A contribution as valuable, for instance, as that from the children of the church - a group where folk are very much beginning to focus on their potential (as in the later chapter by Doug Swanney). When we think of the *Year of the Child* and how much the church gained from that imaginative initiative, I couldn't help reflecting that here was another potential focus group with something to offer. Anybody for 'Year of the Mother'?

Origins and evolution

In one way, the Guild is in itself an old boy's network, the old boy in question being Archibald Charteris, founder of the Guild and much else besides. Reading over some of Dr Charteris's writings, it's scarcely credible that these are historical documents from the century before last. His motivation for founding the Guild was not an inspired 'good idea' to find the women something to do. It did not stem from the theoretical, but was rather a response to some close observation and creative problem solving. His observation was that the church had a mountain to climb in terms of meeting the desperate needs of the people in every parish in the land. What he also saw was a great resource, under-used because its potential was unrecognised; masked and obscured by the conventions of the day. His blinding insight was to realise and declare that the women of the church had practical energies and spiritual gifts to offer, and that they could be a source of mutual support and united action, if properly organised. To post-feminist ears, this is where Dr Charteris goes "off-message". His paternalistic approach does not sit well with us now. We bridle at the carefully worked out structure over which he presided and the firm hand he kept on the tiller of his lively new craft.

But we should not judge him by the current criteria of gender equality. At the time, he was a visionary and, like all visionaries, took the flak from the establishment - of which he was a part, but not a prisoner.

The Guild's most recent publicity leaflet, produced in 2002, reflects the wide range of its interests and concerns, showing people involved in local events, exploring their faith, sharing their resources in support of projects, addressing issues, growing in fellowship. The tag line on the front cover is by Dr Charteris: 'practical energies and spiritual gifts'. It needed no revamping in its description of the group of pilgrim believers that is the Guild, and indeed the Church.

At the General Assembly of 2002, I got uncharacteristically cross with the avuncular Douglas Aitken during one of the lunchtime webcasts. Participating in a discussion of the day's business, I was delighted to have the opportunity of highlighting one aspect of the Guild's report to the Assembly - the question of domestic abuse and the need for the church to respond to what the Scottish Executive had identified as a priority for action. Douglas got it in the neck from me for suggesting that it was something new for the Guild to be interested in 'that sort of thing'. This was a classic case of the image obscuring the reality. The record shows what the Church seems to remain unconsciously blind to: that the Guild has long been developing a manifesto of real Christian engagement with society that goes beyond the comfort zones. That includes support of medical work overseas, outreach work among drug-addicted prostitutes, post-war reconstruction, inner-city poverty, anti-apartheid campaigning, child welfare, debt, sexuality, AIDS awareness, homelessness... the list goes on, as does the commitment. These random examples span the decades of a century and more; and it's interesting to note that some of the early initiatives recur, remodelled for a different time.

In the 1890s country and city guilds were "married", to mutual advantage. There are records of country guilds providing fresh produce for sale at affordable prices on designated market days in the poorer areas of Edinburgh, and of a guild in Glasgow being supplied with '48 garments of good serviceable material, beautifully made with no impossible buttonholes or "anything will do" saving, but the best of shaping and stitching...' In the 1990s, a similar twinning system was revived, and the Annual Meeting of 2002 heard of the prayer support given by Kilbowie St Andrews, Clydebank to its linked guild in Middlebie, Dumfries-shire during the foot and mouth epidemic. Another Guildlink partnership, between Thurso and Aberdeen means that someone hospitalised in the city from the far North need not lack for visitors, nor their relatives for hospitality and support.

No one can doubt the 'practical energies' observed by Dr Charteris, but there have also always been opportunities in the Guild for the development of spiritual and intellectual gifts. Among the earliest intakes of women elders and ministers, many learned to take their first faltering steps in organisation, public speaking and conduct of worship in the supportive atmosphere of the guild meeting. From its early involvement in literacy classes and training in local leadership, to its current advocacy of trade justice and commitment to raising awareness of human trafficking, the Guild has encouraged its members to explore their faith in study and worship and to express it in action. Resource materials and projects in partnership with Church Boards and other agencies afford opportunities for this, but it's important to understand that they do not dictate programmes. So we produce the stuff, but don't expect it to be slavishly followed to the letter - and we regard this as a model for local empowerment, devolved responsibility and so on.

This is an important point. Recently I was approached by a member of a congregation where for several years there had been no guild. A few people had got together and decided they might form one. In my delight and enthusiasm to welcome this new group, I arranged for a package to be sent out to them containing resource material on the current theme, and information about projects the Guild is supporting nationally. This proved so daunting to the small group that they had second thoughts and contacted me again, saying they now wished to withdraw from the national organisation. I had obviously thrown them in at the deep end when they were only at the stage of putting a toe in the water. In the ensuing conversation, it emerged that my offering of *ideas* for programmes and *opportunities* for mission had been seen as "must do's". One by one their concerns were acknowledged and addressed. Support of projects was *not* compulsory; in-depth study of the Annual Theme was *not* obligatory at every meeting. Most important of all, it was made clear that membership of the national organisation was on offer as something the group might enjoy and find helpful in terms of a wider fellowship and focus for service, but that the choice was theirs to make at any time. As it turned out, second thoughts gave way to third thoughts, and that group is now part of the Guild, although they have adopted another name.

Dr Charteris would, in all probability, be appalled at the comparatively anarchic state of the Guild today. My role in the Guild Office is increasingly like that of 'the man from del Monte' who 'say "yes"', as local groups strike out down new paths; seeing a need locally, and looking for some help and guidance on how to fund and implement a modest project that will make a difference in their community. The requests this year alone for grants from the Guild's Initiative Fund describe a picture of a Church thinking and acting outside the box. From island transport needs to the provision of educational resources; from equipment for lunch clubs to training for young church musicians, the grant applications have all included something along the lines of 'what is needed in our community is...', or 'it would make a real difference here if we could...'

But for all his careful structuring of the early Guild, I do Dr Charteris a grave injustice if I paint him as some kind of a control freak. Here's a quote from him in 1893: 'Not the least benefit of the Guild is that, by providing a means of exchanging experiences and suggestions, it has been made far easier for one parish to learn from another; but it does not follow that we must all try the same plans and adhere to the same rules: far, far better that there should be a great variety, as there naturally will be where many minds are trying to supply many needs.' Here's a lesson the old boys' network needs to take to heart. All the carefully thought-out plans for Presbytery reform or review of the eldership, however potentially effective, visionary and sensible, will falter and produce negative reaction if they are presented as 'our solution to your problem'.

The Guild has experience, in a practical hands-on way, of many of the issues of review and reform with which the Church is struggling. How often have I wryly thought, 'been there, done that', when the old boys in the network speak about the importance of consultation, dialogue, inspirational Assemblies, direct appeals for project support, etc. What does it take to get these guys to ask useful questions? Questions like: 'What did you learn from the Research and Development project of the 1990s that led to the restructuring of the Guild?' Is it not just possible that Miss Triggs might have something useful to contribute here - even if it was only what not to wear?

The opposite of paternalism

Learning from one's mistakes, or learning that successes also have their failures, is one important lesson Miss Triggs has learned. In trying to supply the needs of one particular client group, the Guild sponsored an event in the autumn of 2001 under the title 'Time Out'. For several years the number of Young Women's Groups within the Guild had been declining and the rate at which they were disappearing was becoming more rapid. A wide-ranging survey was undertaken in an attempt to discover why these groups were proving less attractive to their traditional membership base. You wouldn't need a PhD in sociology to predict the results. In the main, the former members were not disaffected, they had not been offended by any action on the part of the national Guild leadership, nor had they lost their faith. They were, quite simply, too tired and too busy to turn out to meetings on top of a schedule which typically included, home, family, career and, quite possibly, other voluntary sector or church commitments.

Twenty years ago, when I was involved in one of these groups, it was a lifeline for many women whose lives were bounded by domesticity or full-time work, but not both. The programme could offer relaxation or stimulation, fun or faith-building to meet diverse needs. Now, however, as the younger women attempted what had seemed crazy to their only slightly older sisters, namely the role combination of supermum and indispensable income-earner, it was being revealed that, increasingly, the commitment to the group had become a duty and a burden, rather than a source of support - time to quit.

'Time Out' was an opportunity to take a break from the stress of life as many younger women experience it. The day was held in a hotel rather than a church hall, a buffet lunch was provided, rather than asking people to bring their own sandwiches. Yes, there was a speaker, and a guided meditation on a biblical theme, but the lunch and the exchange of experiences, were the main events. Participants brought items to place on a 'busy' table and a 'calm' table - things to reflect their life as it really is. This was perhaps the most effective statement of the day. No-one had to join anything, no-one had to write minutes or make reports. It was a one-off event with no measurable results. It felt good. I felt good.

Almost a year later, there came a 'phone call. Someone who had been at the 'Time Out' day was ringing to say what a great day that was, and would there be any others? I was able to say that we hoped so, perhaps in a different area of the country. Then she said she was calling to tell me that her group had decided not to be part of the Guild anymore. They were going to go on meeting from time to time, but as an independent group. I was deflated and more than a bit disappointed. A natural reaction? Maybe, but not a particularly healthy one. This is where we really have to mean it when we talk about a church which empowers people to set their own priorities and take their own initiatives. Sometimes their perspective is not ours and we have to live with it.

Life on the edge, beyond the old boys' network, is flourishing. I was revived and refreshed by a visit to the Guilds in Lewis last November. I went there for a weekend of workshops and discussion, along with Marjorie Clark of Christian Aid. Over the weekend we came into contact with some 50 or so women, and a few men, and experienced a warm welcome and great hospitality. Together we followed the programme they had chosen, looking at trade justice through Bible study, domestic abuse through drama, the history of the Guild and one of its recent projects in Croatia, and participating in two Sunday services.

All of this was stimulating and rewarding, but what I will remember most is sitting around a crowded kitchen table, twelve or so of us being fed a generously-proportioned meal as the wind roared outside; those of us nearest the Aga practically toasted from the outside in as the talk ranged far and wide. It was the weekend after the first Sunday flights to the island and there was a robust debate of the pros and cons. Teenagers wandered in and out, sons of our hostess but clearly owned by all. Education was discussed, and local petty crime. A woman widowed young, still grappling with grief and what you do about Christmas and holidays; a retired school teacher with a still sharp mind and a tongue to match if necessary; incomers and islanders; Gaelic speakers and city women. The ministry of hospitality - how crucial and yet how under-rated - exercised in a most gentle, self-effacing manner by a local guild leader whose faith and witness were beyond mere words and smart debating points.

And all around, not a Boardroom table, but a kitchen table - it's a network I'm glad to be part of.

Four:

HEARING THE EVANGELICAL VOICE

C Peter White

Rev C Peter White *ministered in Broomhouse, Edinburgh, for sixteen years, and has ministered to Sandyford Henderson Memorial Church in Glasgow since 1997. He was also Principal of the Bible Training Institute in Glasgow (now the International Christian College) 1990-1996 when it gained accreditation for its own degree course. He is the author of* The Effective Pastor, Mentor Books, *reprinted 2002.*

Does the Church of Scotland have a healthy future? In 2000 we lost 4% of our membership - 460 members a week - a rate of loss which is accelerating. But we are in God's hands and I believe that our future will be bright if, in practical ways, we promote the following seven values.

1. The glory of God

The Shorter Catechism reminds us that our chief end is to glorify God and to enjoy him for ever. Is the key and unmistakeable mark of our worship a people bowed in heart and spirit, in delight and admiration, before God in his glory? The test of worship is not 'was I satisfied?' as though God were made for us, but 'was God glorified?' And the more joyful it is, the more spiritual; the more he is enthroned, the better.

The glory of God is quite as much an 'in the world' thing as it is a matter of our attitude at Sunday worship. As William Barclay's translation of Matthew 5 has it, our light must shine for everyone to see, so that when they see the lovely things we do it may make them want to praise our Father in heaven. 'Our patience and courtesy in stressful situations, our gracious attitude in the midst of difficulty, our willingness to apologise when we are wrong or interrupt our day to help someone. That's called making the boss look good!'[1]

An easy-going minister in Covenanting days decided not to stand out for their principles but to give in to Government pressure. 'What needs all this ado?' he said, 'we will get to heaven and the Covenanters will get no more.' 'Yes,' said the resolute Donald Cargill, 'we will get God glorified on earth, which is more.'[2]

---

[1] *The Word for Today*, United Christian Broadcasters, Stoke on Trent, reading for 12 Feb 2003.
[2] I. Murray, *The Puritan Hope*, London, BofT, 1971, p. 219.

From the same concern, I fear the dishonour being done to God in our national life. Do we stand up for his reputation as we ought? Surely if all 700,000 Church of Scotland members called winsomely for an end of blasphemy on radio and television, for example, it would be significantly reduced in months? After all, think what would happen if the media insulted Mohammed: they would not do it twice! The media moguls take notice of public opinion and I have personally seen courteous protest followed by an improvement in standards in one of our TV programmes. In quiet ways our wellbeing as a nation would be enhanced, I believe, if Scotland gave up using Jesus' and God's name as swear words and revered him again.

2. The saviourhood of Christ

Jesus is a wonderful saviour: let us delight in him! The evangelist D. L. Moody used to say, 'I want to tell you why I like the Gospel. It is because it has been the very best news I have ever heard. No man can tell all that it has done for him, but I think I can tell what it has undone. It has taken out of my path three of the bitterest enemies I ever had' - and he went on to speak of the way the Gospel has dealt with death, sin and judgement.[3] William Tyndale, the Bible translator, said the Gospel made him want to sing and dance and leap for joy. A bit more delight in the saviourhood of Jesus would do us a world of good.

Our Lord is also a necessary saviour: we are told that those who knowingly reject him condemn themselves to eternal separation from God. In that case, let the plight of those without Christ matter to us, and let us offer him to them! Let congregations make regular occasions for explaining the good news. Likewise the great commission, 'Go into all the world and preach the Gospel', is the heart of mission: then let us recommit ourselves in a practical way to the task of world mission.[4] Let us think big about the Gospel; let us 'attempt great things for God and expect great things of God,' as William Carey said.

But what of other religions? We can certainly learn from them. The Muslim praying five times each day, the Hindu's devotion to his temple, the concern of so many of other faiths for the poor and disadvantaged - they can put us to shame. Their zeal for their god or gods, we could do with that. But that is not the same as saying that all religions lead to God. This may be a comforting thought for some but on what is it based? Muslims certainly don't believe it. Nor do Christians. If we follow Christ we follow the one who said 'no-one comes to the Father but by me.'

[3] D.L. Moody, sermon 'Good News,' taken from G. Atkins,ed., *Master Sermons of the Nineteenth Century*, Willet, Clark & Co., 1940, reprinted in Decision magazine, March 1965, p. 6 & 7

[4] Always remembering that we are no longer in a situation where this is simply a matter of crossing national frontiers. 'The missionary frontier runs round the world. It is the line which separates belief from unbelief.' Quoted by J.A. Kirk, article 'missiology' in New *Dictionary of Theology*, ed. Ferguson, Wright and Packer, Leicester, IVP, 1988

When we compare Jesus and Mohammed, or Jesus and Siddharta Gautama, the father of Buddhism, we are simply talking different categories. All were very great men, but Mohammed and Siddharta were only creatures; Jesus is also the Creator. They were sinners; he was sinless. They advised on the way; he is the way. They made no claim to deity; Jesus said 'Before Abraham was, I AM.' People visit Mohammed's tomb; Jesus' tomb is empty. It would be an offence to Islam to worship Mohammed; it would be an offence to the Gospel not to worship Jesus. I hope we shall stand clearly for the uniqueness of our Lord Jesus as God the Son and continue to affirm that he is the one mediator between God and people.

The difference between Christianity and other religions is likewise unequivocal. Hinduism and Buddhism teach that I must pay the penalty of my own sin, if not in this life then in the next, or the one after. Islam too is a religion of human merit; its symbol is a set of scales in which Allah balances your merits and demerits. But the symbol of Christianity is a cross: the work of Christ, not our own good works. In this basic principle - free grace to those who deserve its opposite - Christianity is unique and peerless.

The same principle applies to the issue of inter-faith worship. Does it make sense for Christians who hold at the heart of worship that Jesus was the Son of God, to worship with those who deny that fact? For worship is truly Christian, we say, when it is addressed to the Father, through the Son, in the Spirit.

3. Our need of the Holy Spirit

Believing that without the help of the Holy Spirit we can do nothing, prayer must become a priority again in the lives of individual church members and in the corporate life of the church. In the past in Scotland prayer was at the heart of each church's activities and it must become so again. It is not an activity for the 'super-saintly' or the 'unco' good', but for everyone.

Do people find prayer hard? The disciples asked Jesus, 'Teach us to pray'; and he taught them to say, 'Our Father who art in Heaven, hallowed be thy name.' Teach people to pray if they need to be taught. There is nothing wrong with short simple direct prayers - in fact Jesus himself says so. Praying is not learned in an afternoon but over a lifetime. But we need to start somewhere.

I believe that if there were substantial, united prayer for the activities of the Kirk at both a national and local level many things would change for the better: not only in the Kirk, but in the wider community. And the reason is not hard to find. It is because God answers prayer through the Holy Spirit: granted, not always according to our agenda or timescale, but answer he does. United prayer is also given to us as a significant tool for the achievement of peace and stability both nationally and internationally (1 Timothy 2:1-2).

Especially, we need to pray for preaching. As a preacher there is nothing I want more than Paul's experience: 'I felt totally inadequate but the message came through anyway. God's Spirit and God's power did it, which made it clear that your life of faith is a response to God's power, not to some fancy mental or emotional footwork by me or anyone else.'5 In that case let every member at church on a Sunday, and especially every minister, pray Robert Murray McCheyne's prayer, or something like it, just before the sermon: 'Lord, forgive my sins, grant your Holy Spirit and take to yourself all the glory.' It might seem small, but it honours God, and, if prayed from the heart by whole congregations over a period, I suspect its effects will be, quietly but cumulatively, transforming.

4. The authority of Scripture

The Bible is the hallowed ground where we meet a Father and find ourselves accepted. By the Bible I understand the whole Bible, the Bible as a whole: it repeatedly portrays itself as God's word throughout.6 I want therefore to refute those who would throw out the bits they do not like.

Two friends of mine had a row because one had doubted something the other had said. I'm not surprised he was upset: doubt was being cast on his integrity. For the same reason I still blush with shame at the phrase in a 1998 Assembly report: 'we are not asserting that everything found in the Scriptures is the word of God.' What cheek! Scripture claims to be God's word and we have reason to believe the claim; who are we to decline to take God at his word? Or in Calvin's words, 'to dare to impugn the credibility of him who speaks.'8

I would humbly follow St Paul who wrote to his young colleague Timothy 'All Scripture is God-breathed and is useful for teaching, correcting, rebuking and training in righteousness' (2 Timothy 3:16-17). All scripture, not some, not the bits I like, not the bits I understand, not just the bits that speak particularly to me. We need to regain the spirit of the early translators, like Thomas Cranmer who in his preface exhorted everyone approaching the Bible to bring with him the fear of God.

5 E.H. Peterson *The Message*, Colorado Springs, Navpress, 1995, p. 343.

6 The phrase 'Thus says the Lord' or its like is said to occur some 3,500 times in the Old Testament: E. Sauer, *The Dawn of World Redemption*, Exeter, Paternoster, 1964, p. 11. The OT constantly assumes that it is a Word from God. Jesus said, 'I have not come to abolish the law and the prophets. I emphasise - till heaven and earth disappear not the smallest letter will disappear from the Law until everything is accomplished.' Whenever our Lord was asked about a controversial matter it was Scripture he referred to for the answer. He even called the words of Genesis God's words: *The Creator said,* 'for this reason a man will leave his father and mother ....' The apostles followed him in this, as can easily be shown from every strand of the New Testament. The New Testament was not only recognised as Scripture mostly right from the start, but itself includes testimony to other parts of the New Testament as Scripture: 'Paul wrote with the wisdom God gave him; ignorant people distort his letters as they do the other Scriptures.' There are similar claims, and warnings about ignoring them, in the book of Revelation at the beginning and end.

7 J. Calvin, *Institutes of the Christian Religion*, 1.7.1. Battles trans. London, SCM, 1960, p. 74.

Is the Bible a difficult book? Some parts of it are. Sometimes in preaching I have to say, 'I am not quite sure what this verse (or passage) means. Some commentators think it means this and some commentators believe it means something else. So let's look at both of these possible explanations to see if either or both help us to understand God and faith better.' But most of it is not difficult. 'Let not your heart be troubled...' 'The Lord is my shepherd...even though I walk through the valley of the shadow of death...' 'There is therefore now no condemnation for those who are in Christ Jesus...' And so on. Those are plain enough!

But is the Bible relevant? First ask, relevant for whom? For those who feel far from God? Read the Psalms. For those who are suffering? Read Job. For those who want to know what goodness is, who want to know if there is a God, who want to know if God cares? Read Matthew, Mark, Luke and John. For those who want to know if society can be changed? Read the Acts of the Apostles. For those who want to know how to live a godly life? Read Paul's epistles, and Peter's and John's. All of life is there. The Bible deals with love and marriage, with parenting, with citizenship, with employment, with commerce, with foreigners and our attitude to them, with politics, with congregational life, and so much more.

Scripture needs to be expounded, by which I mean explained (with the help of any and every aid available), and applied. The Bible needs to be covered systematically and methodically so the whole gamut of its teaching is brought into focus for folk. We need the whole Christ from the whole Bible to make us whole people. We need to recover the Apostolic confidence in manifesting Christ who is God's incarnate Word, from Scripture his written word, through expository preaching which is his spoken word. For that is the test of preaching: is the Bible doing the talking, in a contemporary way? Let preaching be expository: it honours God, and God is pleased to honour it.

The late Professor Robert Carroll of Glasgow University, if he but knew it, would be highly amused to find himself quoted by an evangelical in a chapter like this. But to one of his divinity students some years ago he said, 'Stick to the book!' by which he meant the Bible. This advice made the most profound impression on the student in question. This is what we need to do - stick to the book!

5. Changed lives

In what way is the life of a Christian a changed life? First by having a meaningful relationship with God, which in turn produces practical Biblical holiness.

In order to nourish our personal friendship with God, the evangelical tradition has a strong commitment to a regular time - daily or most days, hopefully - listening to God through Bible reading and responding by speaking with him in prayer.

In spelling out the behavioural side of holiness, our Lord reaffirmed the ten commandments bringing out their inner depth, and the New Testament epistles abound with similar exhortation. Take just two examples that are especially contemporary:

'You shall not commit adultery': and amidst all today's heart-searching we have this sure fact: Jesus declared that human sexuality is intended for the indissoluble fellowship of marriage.[8] Hence the whole Bible's prohibition of behaviour which departs from this norm, whether sex before marriage, homosexual practice or adultery. I do not condemn inclinations to other practices; we all experience them. It is part of the glory of God that he welcomes us just as we are, offering us a new start and new power in Christ. The Gospel calls to repentance, nonetheless, all who transgress the Gospel standard.

'You shall not covet': If we lived by this liberating commandment the national lottery would go out of business and millions of ordinary people would be happier, more content and richer. I cannot help wondering also why it is that ministers apply in droves for charges with higher stipends while it is virtually impossible to fill the poorer ones. Are we doing all we can by our stipend structure to mortify covetousness? And shame on Britain for having the widest pay gap between directors and workers in Europe. Other nations manage differently; so could we, given the will.

I do believe we are called to be distinctive in our personal, practical, Biblical holiness. We can and we must turn the world's values upside-down.

6. The upbuilding of God's Church

Christians are not only changed individuals, we belong together in Christ. Fellowship, the active sharing of life in Christ, was an emphatic feature of the early church. Hence the famous and wistful comment 'see how those Christians love one another.' In a world where loneliness, a sense of anonymity and lack of care have been identified as some of the major problems of the twenty-first century, the need for fellowship has never been more pressing.

In our congregation's case there is sustained time of informal sharing after every service, with refreshments and a bookstall and Fair Trade stall after the evening service. We sometimes meet for congregational meals, especially for set reasons such as saying good-bye to our missionaries or as part of contributing to famine relief. Midweek we meet as a congregation to study the Bible and pray together, with part of the time in groups; other churches have house groups for the same purpose. The form it takes is less significant than the importance of encouraging it in whatever way suits each congregation.

In working to build up his congregation Richard Baxter, the English Puritan, developed a practice which some of us have copied fruitfully. In my case after carefully explaining its purpose I invited all members individually (or in couples) to the manse, and we explored three questions over a disciplined 25 minutes: how they came to faith,

[8] Wolfhart Pannenberg: translation by Dr Markus Bockmuehl in *Church Times* June 1996. I have depended on Pannenberg for my whole paragraph. At the point quoted he is expounding Mark 10.2-9.

how they were doing at present and whether they had a giftedness which they would like to use in the service of the congregation. It was among the most powerful pastoral projects I have ever engaged in, and deeply moving.[9]

7. The furthering of God's Kingdom

The kingdom of God arrived in our Lord Jesus, and yet is still to come. Therefore let us work and pray for its full arrival. The Church may be the citizens of God's kingdom, but he rules over all and would have the values of his reign determine all life on earth. In addition to evangelism, therefore, we need to give a lead in the good stewardship of God's creation, to help the needy, to see God's justice done in society; and above all to show in each congregation what a redeemed community looks like in flesh and blood lives and relationships.

This being our calling, it is no wonder that evangelicals have been at the forefront of social good such as universal education and the abolition of slavery and child labour. No wonder that wherever you go worldwide, especially into situations of deepest need, there the mission hospitals, lodging house missions and works of mercy are disproportionately evangelical. I do not imagine that evangelicals have a monopoly on social justice but I do cry out that the Kirk is gravely mistaken to have steadily starved its caring arm, the Board of Social Responsibility, of funding. May we repent of this before it is too late.

The pattern of a congregation's engagement with its wider unchurched constituency will depend on local circumstances. The way to start is an analysis of one's area and one's potential contacts: especially the friends, colleagues and relations of our members. Examples are the provision of a mothers and toddlers group, a befrienders scheme, a teenagers' drop-in café, a youth employment service, a credit union, supper evenings to give young couples a chance to relax without the children, lunchtime seminars in city centres.[10]

In our case, with thousands of students and young professionals as our neighbours, we have introduced an international students café and have started public lectures of likely interest timed to fit the university term. It is important to limit activities to what can be reliably prayed for, led and sustained; this requires pastoral evaluation of the congregation's resources.

[9] W. Benn, *The Baxter model: guidelines for pastoring today*, Northwich, Fellowship of Word and Spirit, 1993. I spell out in some detail Richard Baxter's special, and significant, contributions to the nurture of the church in C.P. White, The Effective Pastor, Fearn, Mentor Press, 2002, p. 125 - 128.

[10] For an exploration of service to the community see D. McAdam, *The Church and Community Involvement*, Edinburgh, Rutherford House, 1992.

These principles - the glory of God, the saviourhood of his Son, our need of his Spirit, the authority of his Word, a holy life in his image, the edification of his Church and the extension of his reign - are characteristic of evangelicalism. Many in the Kirk, whether or not they would call themselves 'evangelical,' will agree with them. The Kirk herself, of course, shares exactly the same glowing centre. 'Cox' comments 'The Church of Scotland is and must remain evangelical in its character, maintaining, teaching and promulgating the great facts of the faith once delivered, in full accordance with the Scriptures, as interpreted from time to time by the ever-living Spirit.'[11]

To hear the evangelical voice is to return to heartfelt commitment to these core values: thus, I believe, giving God the glory he deserves and building a better future for the Church which we love.

[11] J.T. Cox, *Practice and Procedure in the Church of Scotland*, Edinburgh, C of S, 6th edn 1976, p. 6.

Five

THE LAST TABOO?

Jane Denniston

Rev Jane Denniston *is an ordained minister of the Church of Scotland presently employed by the Board of Parish Education as a Regional Development Worker. During her theological training she engaged in research into the Church's attitude to issues of sexuality from a theological perspective, and continues to explore both the theological and the pastoral implications of our theology of sexuality.*

There are many issues in theology over which the Church is divided, yet we maintain life together with little or no threat of schism. For example, women's ordination is a practice with which many disagree but still remain within the Church. Similarly, pacifists and non-pacifists co-exist within the Church without threat of schism. Why then have questions of sexuality, and, in particular the issue of homosexuality, become for many such a defining issue that the unity of the Church may be threatened? For instance, American evangelist and academic Tony Campolo found speaking engagements cancelled when his wife, Peggy, made her support for gay Christians publicly known. This was despite the fact that he neither shares her views, nor was he to speak on that issue.[1] But still, his wife's views compromised his credentials.

The view that 'we have got overmuch into the secular mindset, and…. this is particularly true when it comes to issues of sexual ethics'[2] is undoubtedly shared by many within the Church; but those who struggle personally with issues of sexuality may not necessarily agree. Sometimes secular society seems more accepting than the Church, which can appear to be hostile territory. In the Church the pressures to conform can be immense, giving the impression that everything in the garden of sex is rosy. Thus single people, disabled people and married people struggle alone with their sexual issues, fearing the reaction if they admit to problems. Those who are gay perceive a need to hide a fundamental part of their being if they are to feel, or be, accepted by fellow Christians.

Peter is in his mid-thirties. He belongs to a large city centre church where he is popular and respected. His involvement with charity work is well supported by the congregation, partly because of his personal standing. Peter has known since his teens that he is gay, but apart from a few trusted friends, the congregation does not know.

---

[1] Tony Campolo, speaking at Greenbelt, 2001.

[2] Harry Reid, *Outside Verdict: an Old Kirk in a New Scotland*, St Andrew Press, Edinburgh, 2002, p xxxvi, quoting a minister whom he had interviewed.

Peter feels uncomfortable hiding this aspect of his personality from fellow Christians, but fears the reaction if the facts were made known. Peter, single at present, sees no prospect of celebration if he meets someone with whom he wishes to spend his life. There is neither a real understanding of the pain of his situation or practical pastoral support, as long as he cannot share his deepest feelings within his fellowship. Peter counts himself fortunate to have a supportive, loving and accepting group of friends, but is aware of the potential trauma within the congregation if his true feelings became public knowledge.

John and Margaret are an older couple who have been members of their evangelical congregation for many years. Their adult daughter is actively gay, in a stable and long-term partnership. They love their daughter and have come to a point of acceptance of her orientation, lifestyle and partner. It is a source of pain and loneliness, however, that they cannot share these facts with their fellowship for fear of the response.

In both these situations, loving, open discussion and dialogue would make deeper, closer fellowship possible: but the Church of Scotland has so far seemed to sidestep the issue. In effect, this has allowed a certain liberty of opinion and freedom of expression, a position advocated by the Panel on Doctrine[3]. The fact remains, however, that, in the Kirk, it is unlikely that we will be able to avoid the issue for ever. If and when we debate a theology of sexuality, we should be prepared for a potentially damaging interchange. As the Anglican community discovered in 1998 at the Lambeth Conference debate on homosexuality, this issue may well split the church.

Why this issue may split the Church

That this may be is well illustrated by the Lambeth conference. The discussion was polarised and polemic. Supporters of each position argued their case in language which varied from vigorous to vitriolic.[4] Five years on, the debate still rages as Rowan Williams' recent appointment as Archbishop of Canterbury is discussed. Some object to him, and others support him, on account of his reported views on homosexuality.[5] Such exchanges damage the Church's credibility in the public eye, do nothing to further the cause of the gospel and injure relationships between Christian brothers and sisters. Still, the Church of England continues to debate loudly and fiercely.

3 The Panel on Doctrine Report to the General Assembly 1994
4 One bishop tried to exorcise a practising homosexual man (Newsnight, BBC 2, August 7th 1998), while another was openly angry and critical both of the conservative vote and of individuals who had spoken against homosexual liberation: Ruth Gledhill, 'Liberal Bishop "felt lynched" in gays' debate', The Times, August 7th 1998
5 http://www.royclements.co.uk/links24.htm

Why this should be is a more difficult matter, but it is undeniable that few issues raise hackles as surely as this one. In part it is because the debate raises the question of the interpretation and use of the Bible and how it speaks to our lives in the 21st century. This is a question about which there are strongly held views and so it is understandable that reactions are defensive where it seems that an understanding of scripture is undermined.

On one hand many fear that the Church is in danger of playing fast and loose with the Word of God, interpreting it to suit ourselves and current social mores. Some who take a conservative line on this issue have very real fears that to be more liberal about our sexual morality could be the thin end of the wedge. A Christianity which is constantly reinventing itself may one day cease to be recognisable as Christianity. On the other we have those who find the "traditional" interpretation of scripture oppressive rather than liberating, and personally rejecting. They cannot reconcile this with their experience of God. They find in scripture, and in the experience of the Church through the ages, enough evidence to put a different construct on the Biblical witness.[6]

This, however, is not the first time in the church's history that such positions have been adopted over differing theological or ethical matters Debates on issues such as slavery, the ordination of women and infant baptism displayed similarly polarised opinions. It is therefore no surprise to find them apparent in a debate about sexuality. To many who would take the first point of view, the Bible's stance on this issue is clear: for them its voice is unequivocally against homosexual practice. To those coming from the second point of view, the evidence is far from conclusive. They find nuances within the text, and an approach to interpretation of the text which lead to an understanding of the homosexual state as acceptable to God in a variety of ways.

It is undeniably an emotive subject, but it is hardly surprising that views on whether a sexual orientation is "right" or "wrong" produce heartfelt reactions and an emotional response. Our sexuality is so fundamental to our sense of self that an attack on our opinion can feel like an attack on our person. It should perhaps be said, however, that the demarcation lines in this debate are far from clear. There are those who are homosexual, as well as those who are heterosexual, who are in agreement with a traditional understanding of the Bible. Equally many who argue for a fresh perspective are heterosexual. In addition, although it is too simplistic to talk of two sides since there is a spectrum of belief, the Kirk's Board of Social Responsibility recognised that this is a dialogue which begins from opposite ends.[7] Is it any wonder, then, that it is so divisive? The debate thus too easily becomes emotional and defensive, often leaving individuals

[6] For a discussion of the Biblical issues see: http://www.royclements.co.uk/index.htm; Stuart, Elizabeth, and Thatcher, Adrian, *People of Passion: what the churches teach about sex*, Mowbray, London, 1997; Hays, Richard, *The Moral Vision of the New Testament*, HarperCollins, New York, 1996; Heskins, Jeffrey, *Unheard Voices*, Darton, Longman & Todd, London, 2001; Bradshaw, Timothy, Ed., *The Way Forward: Christian Voices on Homosexuality and the Church*, Hodder & Stoughton, London, 1997; Bell, John L, *States of Bliss and Yearning: The marks and means of authentic Christian Spirituality*, Wild Goose, Glasgow, 1998

[7] Board of Social Responsibility Report to the General Assembly 1994

from every perspective feeling exposed, threatened and rejected. As a result, issues of sexuality threaten to tear our churches apart just as in other denominations the debate on the ordination of women and the abolition of slavery risked doing in the past.

Why should **this** issue split the Church?

Few would suggest that the Church need not address this issue, but many find it confusing that it has become an issue on which to judge orthodoxy, even from a Biblical standpoint.

Jim Wallis, Christian social activist and founding Editor of *Sojourners* magazine, tells of a Bible study that he and some colleagues undertook to investigate a biblical attitude to the poor. One of his fellow students took an old Bible and set to work with scissors, cutting out every verse that related to poverty. When he had finished he had a Bible so full of holes that it would not hold together.[8] A similar experiment which cut out every verse that relates to homosexuality would make a scarcely noticeable difference. Why then does sexuality rather than, for instance, materialism become the benchmark for orthodoxy? An example from the Lambeth Conference of 1998 illustrates a similarly puzzling priority. Delegates from countries like the Sudan were predicting genocide on a scale similar to that of Rwanda and were desperate to lobby their case, but could not do so meaningfully because of the West's preoccupation with sex.[9] More recently, Christina Rees, chair of Women and the Church (WATCH) decided to resign from the Evangelical Council of the Church of England. In the *Tablet* (October 19), she wrote that she had been incensed by the hostility of the Council to Dr. Rowan Williams as Archbishop of Canterbury. In an interview with the BBC she commented, 'The Bible is hostile to usury as well as homosexuality'.[10]

There can be no doubt that, biblically speaking, our sexual behaviour is a matter of moral concern. However, the weight of evidence within the Bible suggests that to make this a touchstone issue rather than, for example, responsibility to the poor, is to risk straining at gnats and swallowing camels. As a Church we may be guilty of finding it difficult to accept one another's views on homosexuality while at the same time apparently condoning levels of consumerism which could be characterised as unbiblical. Jesus' example is not one of monitoring the sexual morality of his followers, although he undoubtedly would have cared about it. He did, however, command them to heal the sick, feed the hungry, and clothe the naked, (Matthew 25:34-46). In his book *Outside Verdict*, Harry Reid shows that he is aware that the issue of homosexuality could divide the Church,[11] yet he is also concerned about the Church's lack of moral

[8] Wallis, Jim, *The Soul of Politics: a practical and prophetic vision for change*, Fount, London, 1995, pp 162 -163

[9] Gledhill, Ruth 'Carey facing his greatest test yet', *The Times*, July 18th 1998

[10] http://www.royclements.co.uk/links20.htm

[11] Reid, *Outside Verdict*, St Andrew Press, Edinburgh, 2002, p 49.

direction in the use of material wealth. He suggests too that promiscuity, whether homo or heterosexual, should be a more significant issue than homosexuality *per se* when it comes to taking a moral stand.[12]

And yet, while the risk of this issue splitting the church is real, thankfully there are many, from the whole spectrum of belief, who believe that the Church needs to talk openly and creatively about this. Discussion can assist understanding and concern, and allows those who may be suffering in silence to receive pastoral care. Furthermore, if in fact our reaction to the issue is based on lack of knowledge, then empathy and understanding can grow when we are introduced to the experience of someone about whom we care. Hence, for instance, many who were against the ordination of women were challenged by meeting women who felt called to ordained ministry. The experience of meeting a different theological viewpoint encouraged a return to scripture. Sometimes there was a recognition that the message of the Bible was not as unequivocal as was believed, but even if the initial view did not change, there was deeper understanding of the issues. This is the kind of dialogue in which the Church needs to engage over sexuality. It is a dialogue, however, which will never take place as long as those who struggle sexually feel they either have to hide the truth about themselves or risk being ostracised, demonised or ejected from their congregations (and there is a sad anecdotal witness to the reality of these experiences within the Kirk). The history of the Christian community shows that it learns and grows in listening to experience. The abolition of slavery, ordination of women, and baptism of infants, are all based on a theology which contrasts the underlying trend and broad principles of scripture against selected and isolated verses. The church found itself developing the theology and doctrine of these issues as a response to the experience of the Christian fellowship. In other words, rather than theology challenging experience, experience was brought to the bar of theology, and it was the theology which changed.[13] For some who consider the Bible's witness to be against homosexual practice this may seem a terrifying prospect, but as long as the Church refuses to discuss the issue in an open and constructive manner, gay Christians will continue to feel alienated, isolated and misunderstood.

With regard to the biblical witness, Jesus never mentioned sex; although he alluded to it in connection with questions of divorce and remarriage. However, his characteristic response to those who felt shunned by their community for whatever reason, was to welcome them, accept them and engage them in dialogue. Think of the woman with the haemorrhage, (Mark 5:25-34); the woman who anointed Jesus' feet with ointment, (Luke 7:36-50); Zacchaeus, (Luke 19:1-10); the Samaritan woman by the well, (John 4:1-30); the woman caught in adultery, (John 8:3-11): all found a response of grace beyond their expectations.

[12] Reid, *Outside Verdict*, St Andrew Press, Edinburgh, 2002, p 174 - 176
[13] The Panel on doctrine report to the General Assembly of 1994 makes this point very succinctly, as regards slavery and the ordination of women.

Is there a way of debating, a language in which to communicate, an acceptance of differing viewpoints which can allow a debate to be conducted with grace? In the knowledge that this is an issue which has the capacity to do deep and irrevocable damage to our fellowship within the Church, is there a place to meet which lessens this risk?

How can we avoid schism?

Sometimes those who enter upon debate do so lacking a real understanding of the depth or complexity of the issues. Peter, whose story we heard, commented, 'I think it is lack of understanding or knowledge that makes people judgemental about anything and this "hot potato" is no different!' The problem exists on both sides of the debate. It is too easy to make assumptions about what it means to be homosexual, and how those who are choose to live their lives. Equally it is too easy to assume that those who come from a conservative viewpoint are homophobic. It is shameful in a Christian church that the content and nature of the comments of a few cause some homosexual people to feel that they have no place in the Church and are unacceptable to God.[14] It is just as shameful that those from a conservative perspective who are nonetheless trying to understand the homosexual predicament can be characterised as 'the anti-Christ' because they cannot accept a liberal gay theology.[15] In a genuine debate, all need to listen. Presently when debate occurs, too frequently the reality is that neither side presents its arguments with the spirit of grace and humility which would encourage the other to listen. The Bible will certainly speak to this issue, but not necessarily as we might expect. This has been the experience of the Church through the ages, and while waiting for the illumination of the Spirit, whatever our stance on this issue, we would do well to speak with less confidence that we are right and another wrong. Jesus understood the people he encountered intimately and so could challenge, rebuke or empathise appropriately. We do not have his perception and knowledge but it is fitting that we should all try to gain a deeper insight into the lives of our Christian brothers and sisters rather than pass judgment. Perhaps more heed should be paid to Jesus' words in Matthew 23:4, where he criticises those who lay heavy burdens on others without themselves attempting to lift them. In dialogue we explore the issues and begin to learn how to lift one another's burdens.

A model for a manner in which such dialogue may be conducted is described by Rev Joy Carroll regarding the debate about the ordination of women within the Church of England. This debate aroused strong feelings in a similar way to the debate on sexuality. She explains how Southwark Diocese organised a "road show" in which the issues were explored in depth: the historical context, the current situation, the case for and against, time for questions and group discussion. The whole debate was designed

[14] For example, an instance reported by David Atkinson in 'The Third Way', December 1995; Also Heskins, Jeffrey, *Unheard Voices*, Darton, Longman & Todd, London, 2001
[15] As reported by David Atkinson in 'The Third Way', December 1995

to be non-adversarial, aiming to be helpful and informative. The objective was to enable people to listen to views which differed from their own in a non-threatening environment. At the end of a series of such road shows it was apparent that understanding had grown, and respect and friendship maintained between people of very different views even in the midst of discussion on a topic which often aroused very deep emotions.[16]

Our faith is relational, based less on what we believe than on who we believe. Remembering the commandment that Jesus gave us to love one another as he has loved us (John 15:12), we have a responsibility to ensure that any debate is conducted in love. The gospel message is that Christians should love and care for their brothers and sisters in Christ, whether or not there is agreement on points of doctrine. In discussion then, the language and approach that we all use can be described no better than in these words from Rev Roy Clements: let there be 'the sensitivity that chooses tactful words; the rationality that offers arguments rather than assertions; the consistency that expresses equal indignation about other social issues; and, perhaps most important of all, the humility to admit that you might be wrong'.[17]

The defining characteristic of such an exchange would be grace. Can we in the Church of Scotland find the grace to listen to one another in humility? Can we find the grace to trust one another to work out our own salvation in the knowledge that none of us are perfect before God? Can we find the grace to trust God to speak to each individual in his own time and in his own way? To be challenging, honing and shaping each of us through all our experiences? So that when we stand before him on that final day he might say to each of us, 'Well done, good and faithful servant'.

[16] Carroll, Joy, *Beneath the Cassock: the Real Life Vicar of Dibley*, Harper Collins, London, 2002, pp 100 -101
[17] http://www.royclements.co.uk/essays15.htm, Roy Clements is a Bible commentator and was a Baptist minister and popular speaker at many evangelical events until he "came out" as being gay.

Section 2:

A Whole People of God...?

Six:

WHAT'S THE PROBLEM? CREATING CONFIDENCE

Iain Whyte

Iain W Whyte *has been the Director and General Secretary of the Board of Parish Education since 1993: he is an Elder at Colinton Parish Church in Edinburgh. A qualified primary teacher with a wide range of experience in community-based and college-based Adult Education, Iain has had a lifelong interest in lifelong learning. In the Church context, he has a deep interest in enabling the Church to benefit from the skills and insights of all of its people. He is also a published composer, with several musicals and a collection of praise songs to his name.*

No-one said it would be easy

Right from the introduction to *Outside Verdict,* Harry Reid identifies a loss of confidence as being at the heart of the Church of Scotland's problems. A lack of clarity of purpose and a sense of fatigue rather than energy characterise the difficulty. The roles of, and relationships between, different offices of the Church - ministers, elders, deacons and others - are muddied and often defensive. The groups that can re-energise the Kirk by working together find themselves beleaguered and suspicious; driven by anachronistic tradition rather than by missionary zeal.

The general tenor of Reid's book, however, is one of hope that the Church can discover again sense of identity and purpose. The difference would be, I feel, that such an identity and purpose would be reflective of today's world rather than some bygone age. A time of plurality and diversification; of a resurgence of sensitivity rather than rationality; of healthy scepticism rather than strong tradition demands a new style of Church in terms of worship, government, authority, and ministry.

I agree with much of what *Inside Verdict* says, but it concerns me that much of what has been written there depends on the views and experiences of people who are immersed in the academic world, or who represent generations that are comfortable with the Church. It is perhaps inevitable that an institution rooted in the modernist views of rationality and structure and logic should be so badly prepared for the post-modern era. Indeed, the academic and rational approach that we cherish may be fundamentally opposed to the spiritual quest that we see in the people of our day.

If that is so, then we have much baggage to lose. Our Committee structures; our

Church Courts, the General Assembly itself, the association with the establishment; all of these may have been strengths of the institution, but now they may be proving to be limitations and shackles.

In this chapter, I will try to consider what the implications are for the Church and how we might begin to change our mindset to one of hope and celebration rather than one of duty and decline.

It's not easy to be a Christian. It's not easy to be the Church. Nobody ever said it would be, and we shouldn't expect it. There will always be challenges and threats and frustrations in our dealings with each other, with society and with God. We need to recognise that what changes over the centuries is not the basic challenge, but the context. Are the results of the changing context - or our response to it - a loss of identity and of confidence within the Church? If the answer is yes, then such losses lead inexorably to defensiveness. We withdraw to a safe place, a siege mentality replacing an evangelical outlook. Caution and constraint replacing courage and conviction. This can be a downward spiral. Insecurity begets defensiveness, begets failure, begets fatigue, begets insecurity and so on. What our Church needs to do is to stand back from its troubles and to look to its possibilities, to accept its limitations and build on its foundations.

As a generation called to be the Church in times of seismic change, we find ourselves all too often struggling to achieve our mission by attempting to hold on to or to recover a (mythical?) golden past. Instead what needs to be done is that we consign our sense of that 'golden age' to the historical wastebasket so that we can move forward with vigour and enthusiasm to be the Church in our day. In other words, when we look back at our past, we should not be trying to copy what our predecessors did in detail and form. We should rather be trying to emulate their astonishing will to do what they saw as God's work in their time and place. To look at the world in which we live and to witness to that world in a Christian way.

Maybe we are like the Israelites in the desert. We have left behind a safe, familiar place (for all its faults) and are fearful of the future. We have heard of a promised land but have never seen it, we are not sure of the route, we are not sure of the distance and so we start to lose heart and to lose patience with God and with each other. Fear; despair; uncertainty; weakness; tiredness; the unknown; loss of identity. Hardly an inspiring collection of allies with which to fight the good fight!

What does this mean for the Church?

So much of the recent thinking in the church centres on a recognition that we need to change. We need to 'learn new ways of being the church'. We need to 'recover the gospel' or to 'stand up for what we believe'. All of this is commendable. But it's also in danger of becoming meaningless navel-gazing if we don't ground it in responsive, prayerful activity. Perhaps we have become strait-jacketed by the kind of mentality that demands change and reformation but cannot deliver it because of vested interests and many other insecurities?

The upshot of all of this is a church that is frustrated and feels sorry for itself in some ways, but which is still too proud and secure in its place in the world to be able to coalesce humility and passion to find itself again at the very heart of society, playing its part alongside, rather than competing with, the other threads in the tapestry that is today's world.

What is our context?

It seems to me that there are three areas (as in all good sermons!) where we need to address our Church lives if we are to recover the confidence of the Church. These are:

1. Within the Church of Scotland itself

2. Within the ecumenical world

3. Within the wider world

Each of these areas could form a basis for discussion and debate that could fill several books, let alone one chapter; but let's have a go anyway.

The Church of Scotland

The Church of Scotland prides itself on being a broad church. It recognises itself as a 'national church' with a unique legal standing based on the preservation of a reformed tradition that dates back to the 16th century, which has seen the terrors of the killing years of the 17th century, with the persecution of the Covenanters, and the struggles of the disruption in the 19th century. We take our place in the long line of the saints; and to think that we will be the last in that line is utterly presumptuous! Instead we need to find the resolve and courage to see our great institution through these dramatic episodes as those before us chose to do. Many have gone before us, many will come after us, be assured of that.

The traditions which we inherit are our strengths. We need to know that. The reformers gave us a Church that has evolved continuously for over 450 years and for us to try to stop changing is to betray them. For us to try recover what they *did* rather than what they *were* is to diminish and insult their sacrifice and their devotion. Let's see them as inspirational figures and not as role models.

This may sound far removed from the life of our congregations, but it isn't. It is by adopting a spirit of change and innovation and by recognising the value of risk that we free ourselves from the introverted agendas that so endanger our work. The reformers caught the spirit of the age, they recognised that the Church and its world are not just linked, they are part of the same weave and we need have no shame in doing the same.

1. If that means we worship in different ways, pray in different words and forms, manage our affairs in more business-like ways, then so be it.
2. If that means recognising the exciting opportunity that information technology, life-long learning, inclusive language and practice can mean, then that's great.
3. If that means changing our structures to meet our vision, then let's do it.
4. If that means recognising the many great achievements that our Church continues to have so that we can pat ourselves on the back rather than beat ourselves up, then we will feel far better about our work.
5. If that means we stop believing our bad news and recognise the force for good that our Church has been and continues to be, then we can be giving thanks to God rather than spending our lives in penance.

The good news in all of this is that there are things happening that tend to suggest not only that such ideas might be valuable, but that they are easily implemented and they work!

The availability and range of music and other aids to worship is probably greater now than ever before. A few minutes in any good Christian bookshop or website will prove that. Diversity, energy and accessibility on every level abound. The awareness of our young people in particular of the possibilities of electronic media is a huge untapped asset. What is more, their expectation of participation in the agendas of their lives offers to the Church a huge well of talent and ability that can only enhance our whole church lives.

Look at some of the things currently going taken on by churches. Multi-media work in places like Bo'ness St Andrew's. Building the life of a congregation around a theme like 'A Disciple Community', as in Colinton in Edinburgh. The contact with over 400 children at holiday clubs like the one at Bourock Church in Barrhead. Youth events attracting over 100 young people in the Western Isles. Our National Youth Assembly. The Year of the Child project. The increasing numbers of candidates for the Readership. The over-subscribed Enquirers' Conferences.

These are the vibrant places in our Church. These are the places of celebration and commitment and confidence and it is by building on these rather than by trying to fix the broken systems of the past that we will progress.

We live in a sound-bite short-term world. That is our reality. We live in a world where leadership and volunteering and sense of duty are treated with suspicion. What we need to do is go beyond the concern that reality gives us and make the contemporary world work with and for us. We need to give people a sense of purpose; avoid giving them a sense of burden. To give people an opportunity to offer what and when they can, rather than bind them around with the stuff of regulation, ordination and structure.

This goes equally for the local and the national organisation of the Church. If we are to benefit from and use the particular qualities and scales that a national organisation can access, then we must address the inhibiting and confrontational limitations of the present structure. We must work to provide a way of working nationally that allows:

1. Ideas to be expressed
2. Risks to be taken
3. Energy to be used rather than dissipated
4. Resources to be channelled to allow national systems to facilitate local witness

To define such a church, we should look to the examples of other places and seek insight from there. The book *The Purpose Driven Church* (Warren, Zondervan) is a "must-read" explanation of the culture shifting and God-releasing change that can happen when we ask ourselves questions about what the Church is for at a given time and in a given place rather than trying to make new wine and keep it in our old and very dry wineskins.

The ecumenical world

As we step outside our own ecclesiastical box, one of the first groups we encounter is the rest of the Christian Church. We in the Church of Scotland face a particular set of difficulties with this: some of our own making and some over which we don't really have much control.

Unfortunately, our ecumenical relationships are often clouded by historical limitations. Our very old story of Protestantism needing to be strict and focussed in the struggle to break free from Rome, or from the Crown, or from patronage, still colours so much of what we do and say. Once again, we seem to take the spirit of our ancestors and mistake it for their actions.

We are not threatened by our fellow Christians. We are called in different places and in different ways to witness before God in His world. That allows us to recognise our differences and, dare I say it, to celebrate variety. As we should celebrate different ethnicities, perhaps we should also rejoice in Christian and religious diversity as part of our thanks to God for the creation of a world of exciting colour and texture.

Implicit within that is a sense of our own identity. One of the problems with ecumenism in Scotland is simply that of size. The relative size of the Church of Scotland compared to other denominations, with the exception of the Roman Catholic Church, is enormous. There is a feeling that any co-operation we are involved in ecumenically can be seen as the Church of Scotland dominating others. Perhaps what we need is a broader view of ourselves in the world church. We are a small part of a huge web and we need to get that in perspective. We need also to know, however, that we are a particular part of that circle. We are part of Christ's body. As Paul said to the Corinthian Church we have been baptised into the one body and we have all been given the one Spirit to drink. To use an irreverent metaphor, we as Scots know very well that one spirit can be drunk in many different ways!

More seriously, though, I believe that we have to know who we are and acknowledge our particular heritage. We need to be secure in it and not apologise for it. Here again, I speak of celebration. We should celebrate our tradition and speak to others in love and with respect, sure in the value of what we know and who we are, confident of our validity within the Church of Christ. We need to place ecumenical involvement in the tool-box of our church. But we must avoid allowing it to become a politically correct and contrived mantra that slows down genuine progress and co-operation.

Indeed, I wonder to what extent the pursuit of ecumenism makes any impression at all on the outside verdict on our Church. Perhaps we need to share a Christian message and to understand our similarities and our differences; but the world outside may be more interested in our sincerity and our ability to be confident in and at peace with our Christianity, than in the make-up of our management committees and the processes of our government.

People value the work of Christian Aid because of what it achieves, not because they see Churches working together. People will see the glory of God and the power of the Spirit in the way we relate to the poor and to the bereaved rather than in the way that we compromise over our business practices.

The wider world

International travel; information technology; plural societies; these are central to the world of today. These and other factors have transformed the world in which we live. What is more, our perceptions and understandings of the world have changed greatly in the past hundred years or so. Two world wars, the death of Empire, the still increasing emancipation of people, have altered the world order in ways that the Church, based as it is on formality and hierarchy, struggles to grasp. AIDS and IT; transient populations; changing demography; the rich, post-industrial west and the emerging, impoverished south, all of these changes leave the church gasping for breath through their enormity and diversity.

The self-confident Church at the centre of a self-confident country has given way to an entity that has more to do with equality, tolerance, understanding and partnership than conquest and patronisation. Equally however, the concerned and conscientious church can easily be overwhelmed by "compassion fatigue" in a world where we see everyone's suffering in its myriad forms on a daily basis in our newspapers, on our TV screens and on our computer monitors.

But we can, as I have said, look at the spirit of the Church rather than the facts. We can use imagination and still keep the light of our tradition burning as a beacon of change, of reformation. We can start, I think, by putting away our insecurities when we meet people from other places and other views. We can stand up and be counted as Christians, without seeing that name as a cloak of spiritual armour to protect us from the infidel. We need to establish our identity and to understand that our way of doing things is just one way of being God's people, but there may be others who express their belonging to God in different ways or who are more likely to come around to ours by seeing and learning rather than by being berated and attacked.

We can fix our point of reference in this tumultuous world by learning about our history and our Church government and our reformed traditions. This means moving towards a church in which learning is secondary only to, and implicit within, worship. In turn it means learning not only about our own tradition, but about others and about the experience of others at home and abroad.

The challenge of the communicating world is to bring us closer to strangers. The opportunity is to learn with and from them and to see more clearly how we fit into the wider picture.

The outcome of that will be to help us work more closely with our neighbours wherever they are and to see service as mission. We need to see ourselves as partners and servants with our fellow travellers. That is not new, indeed it is both the image and the message we have of Jesus as itinerant teacher and open mind.

In Conclusion:

Wad some power the giftie gie us, to see oursels as others see us!

I am more convinced than ever that the fundamental difficulty that we see facing our Church is a crisis of confidence. We are ill equipped for mission when we are saying to people 'We are an ageing group of people, weighed down by fabric problems, financial burdens, difficulty in finding leaders...come and join us!'

We are ill-equipped for mission when we give people the power to deride us and to marginalise us. That won't do. If there are negative views being stated and re-inforced, then it is up to the bold Church to put that right and to accept that people's perceptions of the Church may be wrong in some ways, yet illustrative and illuminating in others.

We are well equipped for mission when we see that our Church is a treasure trove of skills and energy and opportunity, that can be tapped in ways that allow us to serve our parishes and our world and to bring into focus some of the spiritual vision that so many seek.

We are well equipped for mission when we build on our foundations and create new set-ups that release energy from the meeting room and the legal structures, and pour it into worship and learning and service.

Let's think positively. I know pride and complacency are regarded as hugely dangerous, but remember this:

- We are a body of over 600 000 people, around 200 000 of whom gather in our churches every week, and that doesn't include children, visitors and those with us in spirit but bound to home or work.
- We have over 20 000 volunteers working with our young people.
- We have a presence in every part of Scotland and in many other places.
- We have around 100 000 young people in organisations in our churches.
- We have over 40 000 Elders, and many thousands of other volunteer office bearers.
- We have a presence and partnerships in dozens of countries in every continent.
- We are a leading member in the structure of Christian Aid, bringing relief and aid to the poorest of our people.
- We have 1200 ministers; over 350 Readers and 120 Parish Assistants.
- We are one of the biggest charities in Scotland.
- We have over 1000 people in the Guild.

- We turn over in excess of £80 million pounds per annum in members offerings.
- We have members who operate at the very top of many of our largest corporations and in Government.

The list goes on.

Looking back, we have a tradition of education and welfare and service to the whole of Scottish society and the rest of the world, that makes your heart swell with a sense of what God has achieved through this Church of Scotland.

Of course, we can say that the future is less bright than the past - and people usually do - but that can only be addressed if we realise in humility and in faith that what we are custodians of is not a pile of temporal resources, but a tradition of Christian witness of which it is a privilege to be part, and that we are also able to look to the future and see that lineage stretch forward as well as backwards and across our generation.

'Cast your burden upon the Lord and he will defend you,' says the poetry. In practical terms: let's be optimistic and stand full square to the challenges ahead. Let's translate the language of our Church, so that:

'It'll never work' becomes 'Let's give it a go'.

'We tried that before' becomes 'Maybe its time has come'.

'We've aye done it this way' becomes 'So let's try something new, because look where that got us'.

Seven:

LOCAL CHURCH LOCAL PEOPLE:

i) A REVIVING MINISTRY?
(OR... MORE TEA VICAR?)

Susan Brown

Rev Susan Brown *is a parish minister living and working in Dornoch; in her first year on the Board of Parish Education, on the Readership Committee, Susan was previously vice-convenor of Ecumenical Relations - but declined to take on the convenership 'because I couldn't stick my head far enough above the parapet...' She was also on the Special Commission Anent Review and Reform which produced the* Church without Walls *report for the 2001 General Assembly; she subsequently wrote the* Church without Walls Study Guide: Working It Out Together, *published by Scottish Christian Press. She's also one of the local lifeboat crew with inshore rescue (ESRA - East Sutherland Rescue Association).*

The way things are?

Long gone are the days when parish ministers spent their afternoons sipping cups of tea in genteel fashion with their parishioners- if those days ever really existed! What ministers in the Church of Scotland in this the 21st century do, is... well, what is it that we do?

Depending on what kind of a day or week I've had, I might be tempted to suggest that parish ministry is about learning to live with failure. Everyone and their dog, both inside and outside the Church, has their own idea of what a minister should be doing to occupy his or her time; and in reality, no minister can match up to very many of those expectations, never mind hoping to cope with all of them. We can never please all the people all the time and often it seems we can't please anybody!

But that's in my less positive moments. Is it possible though, to be anything *other* than negative given the state of the Church today? The picture all too often being painted of the Church is of an organisation in dire straits. All we ever seem to hear about is how our congregations are ageing and declining; how poor our finances are; how tiny is the trickle of entrants to the ordained ministry; and then on top of all that, we're told that of those who are currently serving in the parish, many of us are virtually paralysed by the great stresses and strains the calling seems to bring with it: all these symptoms strongly suggest, so others tell us, that the Church is dying.

Is that really how things are? It's not how I see things.

I think we're too slow in remembering that the Church is born of a faith which, for more than 2000 years now, has brought hope to people of all ages, in all places - and it continues to do so even at the start of this the 21st Century in Scotland.

That thought is one worth hanging on to, because it ensures that things are kept in perspective. To be honest, although the details may change, I doubt very much whether the problems and challenges we are up against today, differ all that greatly from the problems and challenges Jesus' followers have faced in every generation. What we're facing is a challenge, not to help the *Church* survive... but a challenge to find meaningful ways of living and spreading the Gospel of Jesus Christ at this particular time, in our own particular place, amongst the people with whom we live and work: a challenge that so many in the generations that have gone before us, here in Scotland and throughout the rest of the world, have all had to rise to.

And it is a challenge that lies at the feet of those in full-time ordained ministry, yes, but also at the feet of every one of God's people of all shapes and sizes - and perhaps this is where we need to begin: with ministry as seen in the context of the whole people of God.

For too long we have, I suspect, been guilty of nodding in agreement at the picture St. Paul paints of the Church being the body of Christ, made up of different parts each with their own specific role to play (1 Corinthians 12:14-31). We've read and heard the words about how the eye cannot say to the hand it's not needed and the head not being able to say likewise to the feet. We've got the message that every part of the body is important and necessary and needed and we've *said*, 'See! Everyone is important!' - and then we've carried on letting it seem as though only ministers can really visit, only ministers can really conduct worship, teach, lead meetings, sit on committees and so on. That has to change. In fact it already is changing.

In amongst all the bad news of decline, the Church is recognising that right now she has the richest seam of resources, in the people who sit in her pews - especially, but not exclusively, in the Eldership. Some of these people long to be used, others don't yet know or realise they can be, but in the men, women and children who currently worship and are active in our congregations, there lies the most fantastic potential: a potential St. Paul realised *needed* to be tapped and God *intended* to be tapped.

In the New Testament blueprint for the Church, we're given a very clear picture of the body of Christ as an interactive body: no solo acts, no sleeping partners, instead, all working together for the good of the whole.

It was he (Christ) who gave some to be apostles, some to be prophets, some to be evangelists, and some to be pastors and teachers, to prepare God's people for works of service, so that the body of Christ might be built up... (Ephesians 4:11-12, NIV)

There is an expectation in these words, not that the role of the apostle, prophet, evangelist, pastor and teacher should all be focused and contained in the one individual, but rather that, at God's prompting, *different* people should express the different gifts. And of course, the list of gifts offered is not exhausted in these verses from Ephesians; turn to 1 Corinthians 12:8-11 to read of more.

But how to go about encouraging people to work as a body is the big question - the *real* question. People don't deliberately hide their light under a bushel, they are not intentionally reluctant to offer their time and their talents - often they are quite simply unaware of the gifts they have which God (and in His name the Church) can use.

In Dornoch, that thought led to us undertaking an exercise we called 'casting the net'. Through services, visits and a questionnaire, we tried to help the congregation identify the various gifts every individual has; and we asked them too, to dream dreams: to suggest, prayerfully, what they felt the church should be doing and offering to meet the needs of our local community. Now, again prayerfully, we have the task of trying to shape the worship, work, mission and witness of the congregation around those God-given gifts in the confidence that they have been given for us to use - and to be used in our parish at this time.

And just as an aside - it is amazing how closely the gifts identified correspond to the visions expressed... Watch this space!

The way things could be?

The Report of the Special Commission anent Review and Reform of the Church, commonly known as the *Church without Walls* Report (or CWW) that came to the General Assembly of the Church of Scotland in 2001, made key the importance of this encouragement of the ministry of the whole people of God; it suggested that in order to redress the current imbalance in the way we tend to operate - and in order too, to begin to change mindsets - the term 'minister' should be broadened so that it applies not only to those ordained to Word and Sacrament, but to all those called to live for, and to serve, the Lord.

In giving voice to that thought the Report is echoing the writings of Marva Dawn and Eugene Peterson who, in the introduction to their book *The Unnecessary Pastor: Rediscovering the Call* (p.vii) remind us that: 'there are no higher levels in the life of Christ - there is simply following Jesus and obeying him, day after day, struggling with sin and sinners and being surprised by grace and resurrection'.

While this can be a wonderfully liberating thought for those in parish ministry to hold on to, it can also be a source of stress. For three reasons: one is that while things *are* changing, many in our congregations still crave the 'one-man-does-all' formula; and as a result have certain expectations of those in a parish's full-time employ that are at best incompatible with, at worst downright harmful to, encouraging and engaging the various different parts of the body in working together. One person I visited was irate that when they'd been in hospital no one from "the church" had been to see them. This person had in fact been visited by the Chaplain, by their Elder and by other members of the congregation - what they meant was they hadn't seen the minister...

Secondly, there are parish ministers who, for all sorts of reasons, find it difficult to let others take a more active role in the affairs of the local Church. Fear, the organisational skills it requires, the time factor, can all make doing it yourself seem the simpler and in some cases, the preferred option - even although we know that participation is good and desirable, and an effective way of drawing people in and encouraging them.

And thirdly, with the recognition that *all* are called to ministry, it can become more difficult to define the specific role of those called to the Ministry of Word and Sacrament. If others can preach, if others can visit, if others can teach; if they can lead meetings, work with the young and the elderly, lead house groups and prayer and study groups; if they can and should be encouraged to do all these things- and in many instances do so far better than 'The' minister - then what is 'The' ministry about? What is its distinctive role?

At present the administration of the Sacraments is perhaps the one, single, outstanding distinguishing feature of 'the' ministry - but that function too, is being challenged by a call for Elders, also ordained, to be able to baptise and to preside at the Lord's Supper. And even if these sacramental roles do remain the preserve of the full-time ordained minister, there are parts of the Church where there are no baptisms from one year to the next and the Lord's Supper is celebrated at six monthly intervals. Where then does that leave the Ministry of Word and Sacrament?

Let me quote the CWW Report (13/5 3.1): 'all are called to ministry; and some are called to remind the Church of that, and to *give guidance and focus to the whole Church's ministry*' (my emphasis).

This is a function that is teased out slightly more in the World Council of Churches paper 'Baptism, Eucharist and Ministry' (BEM) as quoted in the above Report: 'In order to fulfil its mission, the Church needs persons who are publicly and continually responsible for pointing to its fundamental dependence on Jesus Christ, and thereby provide, with a multiplicity of gifts, a focus for its unity.'

If I were to put the above into a bite-size sentence it would go something like this: ordination (to Word and Sacrament) gives order to the whole Church's ministry.

The way things should be?

In the innocence and arrogance of youth, when I was asked what I thought ministry was about, I would say that I thought ministry, parish ministry was about doing myself out of a job. Now older and, hopefully a little bit wiser, I still believe that - but I've come to recognise that even the most active, most integrated, most effective congregation (perhaps *especially* the most, active, integrated, effective congregation) needs to have a leader. Not in an hierarchical sense, but from the point of view of ensuring that there is someone in place whose job it is to keep everything in perspective: someone who always has at his or her heart, the bigger picture, the wider vision and most importantly of all, someone who has a strong sense of what the Church is about and whom she seeks to serve.

> 'The chief responsibility of the ordained ministry is to assemble and build up
> the body of Christ by proclaiming and teaching the Word of God, by
> celebrating the Sacraments, and by guiding the life of the community in its
> worship, its mission and its caring ministry.' [1]

But what does all this mean for me as, day by day, I try to work out my calling in the parish of which I'm a part? The God-inspired and created creature which is the Church, needs to be sustained and fed, and this will depend upon a combination of things: the needs, expectations and resources of the congregation itself; the wider parish and, in our case Presbytery, within which it is situated - and the world beyond; and the particular gifts and abilities of 'the' minister.

That means that what might go down well in encouraging the body of Christ in Aberdeen may not be able to do the same for the people in Arbroath; what works wonders in Bearsden may do nothing at all for the people of Benbecula - and that's both the Church's strength and its weakness.

It is not possible to lift and transfer a recipe for success from one congregation and impose it on the next. There is no single, off-the-peg formula for success that any congregation can order or pick up and cloak themselves in and everything will be guaranteed to go well. Each congregation, each parish, has, under the guidance of the Holy Spirit, to find its own way to live out and to live with the Gospel in the area and with the people in which it lives and works. And that is not the same as saying each parish stands alone - it's exactly the opposite. It's reminding us first of all, that the faith we hold on to has to be applied: and it's reminding us too, that the Body to which we belong is always much greater than the sum of any of its parts - it's reminding us that there are others around us who are about the same business we are, our Father's, and therefore there is the opportunity to work *with* those others to the greater glory of God. Others within the Church of Scotland... *and* others across the denominational boundaries.

[1] *Baptism, Eucharist and Ministry,* World Council of Churches 2000 13/14

All this should serve to make us realise that the success of a congregation (or the success of a ministry) should not and cannot be measured by the number of people it has been possible to insert in the various boxes of the Church's pro-forma annual statistical returns, or by the amount of income the congregation has generated, or even these days, by the number of people who turn up on a Sunday morning: but by how well that congregation manages to relate something of the Gospel to all the people around it - seven days a week, through word *and* action.

Which takes me to what, the more I think about it, is probably the bottom line of my ministry. It is about encouraging relationships. The relationship first and foremost with God the Father, through his Son with the help of his Spirit, but integrally bound up with that is the encouraging of relationships one with another both inside and beyond the church walls.

And there are many congregations the length and breadth of Scotland who are already totally committed to doing exactly that: there are many congregations totally committed to encouraging and nurturing healthy relationships. Some are showing that commitment in big, dramatic ways through their support of inventive and sometimes adventurous projects and programmes, within and beyond the church buildings, and others are showing it in quieter, perhaps less news-worthy ways, by creating links with others on a much smaller scale - even one-to-one. Whichever way congregations go about it doesn't really matter - what *does* matter is that it *is* happening, because this relational activity, to me, is central to the life of the Church, the body made up of many parts called to be the body of Christ.

Throughout Scotland, at God's instigation, under the leadership of 'the' minister, working with the skills and gifts of all the ministers who are the whole people of God, congregations are regularly and actively looking at ways in which to forge new relationships with one another, with their local community and beyond and they are looking too, to strengthen existing relationships. Which is totally in keeping with Christ's command to 'love the Lord your God with all your heart and with all your soul and with all your mind... (and) love your neighbour as yourself.' (Matthew 22:37-38)

And perhaps surprisingly, that seems to take us back to the cup of tea with which we began. Sitting down with people, where they are; talking, listening, making time for them as God has made all the time in the world for us, building up relationships on every level...

Maybe it's not such a bad idea after all! One lump or two?

ii) SMALL FACES, BIG LIVES: UNLIMITED POTENTIAL

Maureen Leitch

Maureen Leitch has been Parish minister of Bourock Church in Barrhead for last seven and a half years; she entered ministry after having taught in secondary school for 16 years. She has served as Convener of the Community Interests Committee for Paisley Presbytery, and is Convener of the Barrhead Christian Aid Committee. She is the Convener of the Eldership Committee of the Board of Parish Education.

The church began as a movement driven by a vision. It consisted of small groups of people who believed that Jesus was the Son of God and who had committed themselves totally and unreservedly to him as Lord and Savior.

These groups replicated themselves throughout the Mediterranean world and beyond. They had no real estate. Their leaders were, for the most part, local people whom the apostles appointed and empowered. The movement had no social prestige or influential patrons. It operated from the margins and succeeded in infiltrating every level of society and department of life.
(Eddie Gibbs: *Church Next,* Inter-Varsity Press 2000 p.234)

The Church today...a tale of woe?

That description above seems to be light years away from the church we see today. The church beginnings seemed to be driven and confident despite the fact that it was on the margins and had no real power behind it in social terms. The emphasis was very much on work at a local level and it must have been seen to be worthwhile because it replicated itself throughout a large area.

Perhaps we don't recognise the present Church of Scotland in that description because much of our work seems to be centred on maintaining the institution and meeting the needs of existing members, rather that going out into the community. Whilst both these functions are important, they must never be regarded as the only functions of the church. Perhaps it could be argued that the church was at one time a power in society, but the case could be also made that today the church is no longer in the centre of society and is drifting inexorably towards the margins. If it did have power socially at one time, this would seem to be very diluted in these days. For example, the church was very influential in setting up the education system in Scotland and at one time Christian Education was a requirement at all ages; but now, the church has little influence in a secular education system and Christianity is but one part of the subject matter of Religious, Moral and Philosophical Education. At one time, moral issues such as co-habitation before marriage and divorce were heavily influenced by the voice of the church; but today, that is not true. It would seem to be fair to say that modern lifestyle is considerably less influenced by church thinking than in the past.

Today then, has the church has lost some of its vision? Has it become so inward-looking that it has lost its purpose of mission? Is it in decline? Has it let its vision be taken over by the few who are styled 'leaders' - by this, I mean those who assume roles which give them the power to speak on behalf of the church e.g. Conveners of Boards, Directors of Boards, or the Principal Clerk? Do the people in the pews really care about the seeming decline? These are some of the questions that many have agonised over in the past few years in trying to discover what "church" means in our society today.

There are many tales of woe about the state of the church, and it is easy to get caught up in the negative cycle of thinking. Indeed, at times it would seem that everything in the church is doom and gloom. Both in the secular world and within the church itself, it is difficult to detect positive vibes about the future. However, it must be said that there are many tales of celebration and achievement - but, of course, they do not make such interesting press, so we rarely hear about them.

Yet, we need to hear them; we need to be encouraged by them; we need to celebrate them. Indeed, the world at large needs to hear them too, so that the negative image of the church is changed. If you don't believe it has a negative image, just watch your television and see how it is portrayed in the 'popular soaps'. The stories are never of celebration and achievements but more of prohibition and doom-laden messages. By and large, the tales of joy and celebration are the stories of local congregations and what they are attempting to achieve. They are the stories of how the church in its local context reacts to its community, and reaches out in diverse ways in love and with a vision. They are stories of churches making a difference to the lives of those who are in the local community and who need some kind of support.

"Being church" is local

It is my belief that if the Church of Scotland is to survive and thrive in the future, it needs to acknowledge the importance of local congregations and the saving power that lies within them. Although most local congregations would probably minimise their own importance and regard themselves as being "small faces", there is no doubt at all, in my mind, that they have "unlimited potential".

Indeed I would suggest that the local congregation, where the members meet to worship, to enjoy fellowship and to be strengthened to be as Christ to the world, is the powerhouse of the church. Often it is assumed that the powerhouse of the church is

121 George Street and its outlying departments, where the General Secretaries and their staff work or, alternatively, the Boards and Committees with their Conveners and numerous members - and I hasten to add that I don't believe that those who fill these positions think any such thing! Sometimes assumptions just grow round vague ideas perpetrated by a few misguided people.

It strikes me that, at times, we have managed to turn around the whole idea of 'being church'. The congregation feels as if they are there to serve the minister instead of the other way round. Local congregations feel as if they have little importance and are there to serve the Boards and Committees when, of course, the reverse is true. Boards and Committees are made up of people from local congregations who are there to represent local views; but somehow, the person in the pew does not perceive this to be the case. They tend to regard them as 'superpowers' who make decisions from 'afar'.

The Church of Scotland seems to get caught up in 'political' manoeuvres which assume an importance that has no resonance in the local parish church... in fact, I would go as far to say that the average person in the pew has little or no interest in these machinations. Let me take an example. The church gets into a real 'tizz' about who will be elected as Moderator of the General Assembly... it causes great debates in certain circles and some become quite heated about it... yet for most people in the pews it is an irrelevance because it does not impact on them.

I am not saying that we should do away with these structures: rather I am suggesting that we concentrate less on them and more on the work that is ongoing in our local congregations. For it is there that we will find most to celebrate. It is in these places that the doom-merchants should really take an interest, because there are real signs of life and growth in these gatherings.

What might someone find in the local church situation?

- A group of people who are open and welcoming, particularly to the stranger in their midst.
- People who enjoy worshipping together and show that to be the case.
- People who not only listen to the Word of God, but engage with it and go out and act on it.
- People who are innovative in many different ways.
- People who care.

These people will react to situations in appropriate ways. For example, those in the community who are bereaved can find support and solace within the local church. Many have been surprised to be welcomed and comforted after a bereavement. It may be that this sad event has brought them into contact with the church for the first time in many years. They are always grateful and surprised at the comfort and support offered.

I think it sufficient to say that the diversity of talents on offer usually means that someone naturally reacts to whatever situation comes into the church. As a minister, I feel that I am greatly blessed to work alongside so many wonderful and loving people.

The potential of the local church

I don't think my church is any different from any other church. It is my contention that every local church has a wealth of potential within its ranks. Every member has some gift or talent to offer. If this talent can be utilised to the maximum effect, the power of good that can be released is unlimited. This is no new revelation... it has always been the case. So why bring it up now?

My reason for doing so is that I believe that our mind-set about 'being church' needs to be changed. For too long we have equated church with its leaders, rather than with the people in the pews. My contention is that over the centuries we have become too minister-oriented... we rely too much on the figure-head person. The more we rely on the minister the more we under-use the gifts of the people. Not only that, but the more we rely on the minister the less effective he/she will be... the more burnout is a possibility.

It has been suggested that if we produce more great preachers we will save the church. In other words, if we get more people who can stand in the pulpit and hold people's attention for 20 or 30 minutes that will save the church. I would dispute that.

Yes, we do need good preaching - but it must be preaching that evokes action. It needs to inspire the people to go out and spread the good news. It is not great preachers that will save the church - it is great people! The church will not be saved by that half-hour preaching on a Sunday but by the other 160+ hours in the rest of the week. It is then that the 'people' will 'be the church in action'.

The church will be saved by those who fill the pews - not by those who fill the pulpits, and not those who make up Boards and Committees. The job of 'being church' falls to those who are grounded in and want to serve their local communities; those who can identify the needs of their community and then be prepared to go out and meet that need. It is those sitting in the pews who can go out and be 'as Christ' to their neighbours. They are the ones who can serve their community in so many different and meaningful ways. They may be 'small faces' who will never have any national recognition, but they are the ones who will make a difference.

It is also those who are grounded in their nation who care enough to bring a Christian perspective to its policies and laws. Church members can affect policies, if they care enough they can have a strong voice that does impact on our politicians.

It is those who are grounded in their world who want to campaign for justice and debt resolution, and whilst working for that will do what they can to help those in need. Campaigns such as Jubilee 2000 (which campaigned to end Third World Debt) had a big impact, and many, many church members were actively involved in petitions, in sending postcards to MPs and in attending demonstrations.

These are the kind of people you will find in the local parish church. The 'ordinary' person who, inspired by the teaching of Scripture and inspired by the Holy Spirit, becomes anything but 'ordinary' - indeed, becomes 'extra-ordinary'. Our churches are full of them. This surely is a reason for celebration. If we take a look all around Scotland, will we find another organisation which offers its community such diverse activities as:Toddlers Groups, Summer Clubs, Youth Organisations such as Boys Brigade, Girls Brigade, Guides, Brownies, scouts, Guilds, Men's Clubs, Choirs, Discussion Groups, Bible Study Groups - and many, many more?

Many local churches do their best to do all of this, and most of it for free because willing volunteers offer their time and their talents. In terms of Social Capital the impact of the local church is often underestimated. Most communities would be poorer if the local church did not offer their facilities and talents to the wider population. My own church can run a Summer Club for somewhere in the region of 300 local children. This requires some 70-100 volunteers. We do get some help from people in other local churches, but the vast majority is drawn from one church. These are all busy people, yet they are willing to give of their time and talents to serve the community. In today's climate of self-seeking and building one's own 'empire', this kind of service is to be praised. All over our country other people are doing the same in their own community. These are the kind of stories we need to hear. We need to recognise the breadth and the quality of work and support that is being offered in Christ's name.

On these building blocks - of ordinary people in touch with the needs of their community and, inspired by the Holy Spirit, offering their abilities - we certainly should be able to build a church that is relevant, living and growing. Instead of bemoaning the "state of the church", I would like to see us acknowledging our strengths and consolidating them. Some will argue that the church is in decline because the number of members is falling year by year. This is true in that, statistically speaking, there is a decline. However, it may be that this provides an opportunity for growth in other ways. A leaner church just might be a more efficient church. Smaller numbers may just allow for the identification of the talents which lie in the congregation, and for the encouragement to use them. We need to move away from being caught up in the 'numbers game', where we judge success only in numerical terms.

The vision must be local

Perhaps there is some sense in reclaiming the kind of church that we had at our beginnings, as described by Eddie Gibbs (see above). A church that had no power or social standing; a church that had little bureaucracy; a church that used the talents of the people; a church that, nevertheless, did influence people and did grow.

The power in this church lay with the people and the strength came from their belief in the Lord Jesus Christ as their Saviour. The local parish church today needs to reclaim that power and be enabled to share their beliefs with others. This kind of empowerment will only come when we start recognising 'local' solutions for problems rather than trying to fit every church into a national template of solutions.

It is my strong belief that the time has come to start celebrating what we have in the church today, and stop concentrating on what, perhaps, is seen as the 'glory days of the past'. New times bring new challenges, and we have the resources to meet these challenges. These resources have lain largely 'untapped' for far too long. Let's wake the sleeping giant. Let's stretch our congregations to see what they can achieve. Let's return the power of decision-making to a more local level.

It may be stating the obvious, but I just have the sneaking feeling that if you centralise decision-making then those 'small faces' in the congregations feel that they have no power, and play no real part in the decision. They increasingly feel that decisions have to be made by 'experts', and therefore they do not qualify. Yet, we need to hear these voices. They may be 'small faces' unrecognisable from their neighbour in terms of the national church, but they are not 'small minds.' My feeling is that we need to let them decide what is best locally and use their knowledge of the local situation.

Let me make a plea that we allow our local congregations to recapture their own vision for their local community. 'Where there is no vision, the people perish' (Proverbs 29:18, KJV). Our congregations must be encouraged to work out their own vision for the local community. This may necessarily have to be in conjunction with neighbouring congregations, but can be so much the stronger for that. The potential we can unleash is unlimited. Of course this does not mean that there is no role for ministers or those employed by the church as advisors/specialists. They need to be the facilitators and enablers. However they must resist the temptation to take over.

The vision must come from those who are grounded in their community. They are the greatest resource which the church has. They are the church's greatest wealth. They should also be the biggest cause of celebration.

I admit that I am looking at this from the inside of the church. From that viewpoint I am not dismayed. Yes, the church is changing - perhaps it is more marginalised than it has ever been in our country. That only brings a sense of challenge and a will to use the resources at our disposal to make it meaningful in its local setting. As long as we have 'small faces' who are willing to show their belief in Christ by their actions in the world I think we can go forward in positive and joyful mood.

Conclusion

Eddie Gibbs in the quotation above talks of the early church 'operating on the margins', but notes that this church 'infiltrated every level of society and department of life'. Perhaps that brings both an affirmation and a challenge to us today. We can be affirmed that although we are now 'on the margins' of society, we are not the first to be there, and the early church grew from just that situation. We are challenged because we must explore how we can be influential from where we are. There is little value in hankering after days gone by. We must be prepared to accept that 'here we are, back on the margins' but we are ready for something new happening. We must prepare for re-birth: and that will mean changes in structure, the identifying of giftings and the enabling of such, to provide the church with new ministries.

We have the talent, we have the resources and, in many places, we have the will. It is from churches who are prepared to have a vision for the future and work toward it that new life will come. These churches are not afraid of change. Such churches will have an impact on their communities and these are the ones which will move the church from the margins back into the centre of society. These are the churches which are beginning to unleash their potential in their own local setting.

Section 3:

Church of Tomorrow or Today? The Age-old issue

Eight:

CHILDREN FIRST

Doug Swanney

Doug Swanney has been working in Children's Ministry with the Board of Parish Education since 2000. Previously he studied at Glasgow University and Union Theological Seminary in New York, gaining a Masters Degree in Theology. A volunteer Children's worker in local parish churches for fifteen years, he has lead numerous Summer Clubs and has recently finished a writing project for Scripture Union. Doug has been co-ordinating the Year of the Child project for the Church of Scotland and is continuing with this work through the Children's Forums around the Kirk.

As a child growing up in the Church of Scotland, I recall being taught that pride was a sin. You were not meant to feel boastful, or big-headed about those things you had done well in your life. It has perhaps always been the Presbyterian way to focus on those things that we do not do well, the things that we can claim to have failed at, that become much more of a focal point for us. This may explain why most Presbyterian worship tends to have a larger emphasis on confession than on thanksgiving! Although I am not going to assert that we should be boastful about certain elements of the life of the Kirk, I will however claim quite openly at the outset of this chapter, that the Church of Scotland has a unique, strong, and impressive history in children's ministry. Not only that, but that we see around us many of the signs of growth in children's ministry that would indicate the probability of an exciting future ahead.

The Kirk has long had a special place for children in its life, and as we become more aware of the need to offer children equality and involvement, this special place for children is becoming more important. Our Church is great at children's work, we have thousands of children involved and committed to the life of the Church, and that is something about which we should feel extremely confident and pleased. From traditional models of educational delivery to innovative ways of enabling children to engage with the gospel, the Kirk is a flagship for children's work.

Bold claims? Indeed! The gospel of Jesus Christ teaches us many things, one of which is to speak the truth and to make claim to the kingdom that has been promised. In the continuing growth of children's ministry, I see the kingdom coming and the realisation of many years of dedication to and from children.

page 68

Working for the Church is a great privilege. Week by week I am continually impressed and heartened by the stories of the work that goes on across Scotland, England and Europe in our parishes and congregations. Many of our members believe that children have so much to offer the Church, and will continue to stretch the boundaries with new ideas and initiatives, and that is something worth shouting about.

In this chapter I would like to explore four areas within children's ministry in the Church of Scotland that I feel give us all the evidence we need to thank God for the places where children's ministry is growing; as well as making us all think again about the ways in which we need to continue to improve and embolden children's ministry. Through the areas of Church, Holiday Clubs, Activities, and Faith, we shall go on the journey that represents some of the best of the Kirk's children's ministry.

A Church for children, and a camel through the eye of a child

Our Church has a great tradition of education and commitment to learning for children. Historically the Church's influence is evident in the education system we see around us today. The parish school was where children from all backgrounds learned to read and write, and such schools were the precursor of the idea of education for all that we enjoy now. As the country changed so the Church evolved and offered instead 'Sunday' school - a place where particular learning about the gospel and the history of God's people took place. As society has changed, so the look of these Sunday Schools has changed. More and more churches have now 'junior churches', places where learning takes place alongside worship and service. These junior churches offer both teaching and praise, and are staffed by some of the most committed and innovative volunteers you will ever meet. Week after week there are thousands of children involved in these gatherings, many of which employ the most up-to-date teaching methods, as well as using IT to back up the learning experiences. Gone are the days of worn-out felt tips and old wallpaper for drawing: these days, many churches would rival some of our schools for the materials and methods employed to ensure we are teaching our children in the best way possible.

These junior churches are seen as being an integral part of the whole life of the church, not just as a place where children go so that the real worship of the church can begin in earnest. The junior church is not just another congregational organisation and gives freely of its life to the whole parish. Many junior churches have children who attend without their parents; young individuals who get up on a Sunday morning and make their way to Church because they like it, because they feel part of the community. Our junior churches continue to be an important part of the education life of children in Scotland, and should be supported by our Kirk Sessions in both prayer and finances.

These changes in the way that children learn is also reflected in the changes that we can see in the time the children spend with the rest of the Church community. For many of our churches the issue of 'noisy' or 'disruptive' children is thankfully something that has been resigned to the annals of history. This has been done because worship has ceased to be something that we "do to" our children, but something that have an involvement in, and something that they truly enjoy. It is not yet possible to say that this is the case in all our Churches, but the vision has been articulated by the children of the Church for a better way of being community, and as more Churches grasp that and let the children lead them forward then the more whole will our worship be.

The 'Children's Address' is often one of the markers that people use to define a 'good' Minister - the cleverer the props, the louder the laughter, then the more the Minister is applauded for 'being good with the weans'. But a good children's address is not about laughs, or clever props; many of our Ministers have realised that this time is about relationship-building with the children in their care, a time for reflection and teaching. Children are brighter than we think, they see through the props, they see through the questions - as the old, old story about the Children's Address tells, many of them know the answer will be Jesus before they are even shown the picture of the camel! Churches have come to realise that children want to be involved, to enjoy their life in Christ, and not be patronised, or used as the butt of easy laughter for the adults.

It is heartening to visit many churches and see Minister and worship leaders involve the children in discussion and reflection during the service, as well as enabling them to choose the children's hymn, lead prayers, and share the readings from the Bible. One of the most amazing learning experiences I had (and there were many) from the work of the Children's Forums, during the Kirk's Year of the Child, was that the children in our Church were not asking us to make the service all about them, or use only the music that they liked. All through the Forum process they talked about compromise; about ensuring that Church was something that all ages could relate to. For them this meant that there had to be mix of music, a mix of prayers, and an understanding that some bits of the service may not appeal to everyone but that does not make it boring or irrelevant.

For instance, many people were astonished to discover from the Children's Forums that the children did not always want to have the Praise Band leading worship. Not only that, but they acknowledged that the organ and the old hymns had a real place in the Church. They reason they gave for believing this was, they said, because the old hymns were nice for the older people, because they were what they sang when they were children, and so they shouldn't be deprived of these memories. That kind of compromise could well be something that many in the rest of our Church could learn from!

In our sacraments we have also changes that herald this new age for children in the Church. After years of discussion the Kirk's General Assembly finally decided that children could be permitted to take part in communion in 1992.This permission was provisional, depending on whether the Minister and the parents were satisfied that the child understood what the communion was about. This task was seized on by many of our churches, and in a spirit of optimism, a good number of parishes have pushed ahead to ensure that 'Communion Sunday' is not a Sunday for the children to stay at home because there is nothing for them at church. For instance, I was delighted to see the work of one particular church, Wallneuk North in Paisley, where the children's leaders had produced a whole teaching programme for the children to take part in before they attended Communion. After seeing this I wondered if we would soon be in a situation where the children would have to be teaching the adults all about Communion! Many churches still struggle with the issue of Communion; but the important issue is that they are struggling with it, rather than ignoring it. Many churches involved children in special Communion services for the Year of the Child: in these services, the children not only took Communion, but they wrote and led prayers as well as serving the Communion to the rest of the congregation. Many people reported that these services were among the most moving Communions they had ever attended. As the Lord's Table is opened to more and more children, so will the faith and commitment of these young worshippers grow; and that can only be of benefit to our Church and to the work of the Kingdom.

Baptism continues to be a central sacrament for the Kirk, and Churches continue to take this responsibility seriously. I know of a number of churches who now have an Elder responsible for Baptism; who visits the family along with the Minister, and continues to stay in touch with the family after the baptism. As we bring new members into our church through Baptism, these young additions to our family may seek to learn, to praise, and to serve the Church they belong to. We will only see these fruits of Baptism if our communities are willing to accept children and enable them to live a life of faith. Where we stand in their way, we stop them from developing.

It is not changes of ethos we see, but also changes in the material surroundings of our Churches. People have begun to discover that many of our buildings are not suitable for the all-age worship they are trying to create. Pews that children cannot sit on or see over, chancels that do not lend themselves to the kind of work we do with children, nowhere for prams and buggies, no provision for baby-changing: these are just some of the things that churches have tried to address. The introduction of soft-play areas, for example, has created a space where young families feel welcome rather than tolerated. The changes are ones that signal a move, one that is centred on Jesus' call to bring the children to him.

Holiday Clubs R Us

The second area of growth and real promise I would like to look at is that of Holiday Clubs. If I was a tabloid journalist I would headline this, with something like, *Holiday Club Phenomenon Sweeps Kirk* - but instead I *will* say that the provision of Holiday Clubs is one of the real growth areas of the Kirk. Research undertaken by the organisation, Christian Research, commissioned by the Board of Parish Education for the General Assembly of 2001, showed that there were almost 50% of churches carrying out a Holiday Club in some form or another. Many of these Holiday Clubs find their roots in the old Summer Mission format and some are still supported by the Board of National Mission's Impact teams. Many churches have entered into this venture because they take their responsibility to the children of their parishes, and to the call to mission, very seriously.

If you travel around Scotland during the Summer Months, you will see many of our Churches displaying banners and posters, advertising mind-boggling weeks such as 'Desert Detectives', 'Groundbreakers' and other exotic titles. Although these weeks are all themed in a variety of ways and are dressed up very cleverly, they have at their heart the story of God's salvation of the world. These weeks have become the strong foundations of many churches' children's programmes, and bring together an inordinate amount of talent to make them happen. What is more significant is that these events are not just about the children that attend - they say much about the community that is created to make them happen, and that involves all ages. Two summers ago I was amazed by the commitment of two ladies, more mature members of Penilee Church in Glasgow Presbytery, who decided that they would run a Holiday Club; and that age was no barrier to what they saw as God's calling to them. And this story is repeated in many places. The Holiday Club is fast becoming a central part of mission-work to children. Churches regularly have children gathering in their hundreds - yes, in their hundreds - to praise, celebrate and learn about the word of God.

The Holiday Club is a tool for congregations to grow together as they work together. It can be the catalyst for changes in the life of the whole Church, and is something that all churches should consider doing. Apart from benefiting the life of the host congregation, it looks outwards to the parish and opens up a conversation with potentially all the children and young people that are around. Perhaps in the years to come, we will see more funding be made available for this work both at a local and a national level? Putting our money in the projects that really are working for the Church should be a chief priority, surely.

Children and the commmunity

The third area in which we can see the continued success of the Church in this area of work is in the many activities that we offer, or which are connected to the life of the local church. On doing initial research for the Kirk's Year of the Child, we found that the provision for children across the Church was a real cause for celebration. From breakfast clubs, homework clubs, mid-week fellowship, youth choirs, drama groups, to the more traditional uniformed organisations, the Church of Scotland could probably claim to be one of the chief providers of services for children in Scotland. Through these many different activities, children are in and around the life of the Church many more days of the weeks, and for more hours, than most of our adult members. And for the children these activities are important, and are part of a life that contains many choices of how they can spend their time. When the children come along to these church activities, it is not because there is nothing else to do, it is often because it is central to their lives.

These are not just activities that benefit the children, but are tied to initiatives that act as a service to the whole community. Children in the Church are involved in supporting pastoral work, fund-raising for many charities, as well offering their talents in worship. One activity that had a huge impact on many churches was the introduction of the Children's Forums during the Kirk's Year of the Child. These groups of children committed two years to a process that involved them in meeting every two months to discuss matters relating to the whole work of the Church, at both a local and a national level. They had input into the National Debate on Education, the discussion on Religious Observance in Schools, and also the Child Protection Review, all carried out by the Scottish Executive. The children involved in these Forums opened up their hearts and minds, and shared with each other their thoughts and hopes for their Church and their country. These thoughts have gone on to shape the future planning for children's ministry.

In turn, these Forums elected and sent representation to the General Assembly of 2002. For the first time in the history of our Church, the voices of those under 16 were listened to, and considered by, the General Assembly. What was significant about that was not only the way that the children presented their own views to the Assembly but the way in which the Assembly received them. After some initial apprehension of the Children's visit, they were welcomed joyfully by the Assembly, who received their report with warmth and gratitude. That one single event changed the life of those children, and of the Church of Scotland, in a way that could never have been imagined. The ongoing result is that ways are currently being explored that will ensure that children can always have their voices considered by the General Assembly. This, along with the fact that many Kirk Sessions now hear from the children, in the congregation and outwith, through Forums, means that the notion of being 'seen and not heard' is as dead in many places as the outdated thinking that led to children being seen as 'the future of the Church' - rather than the Church's 'here and now'.

Children of faith

The last area that I wish to highlight is perhaps the most important and the least tangible. So far we have looked at the concrete impacts that children have on the Kirk, but there is something far more important in the lives of the children of the Kirk that we need to celebrate - their faith. Through the children that I work with in my home Church, I am continually amazed and in awe of the strong beliefs and commitment they can bring to their faith lives. I have witnessed children speak out to friends about their love for Jesus. I have seen children attend bible studies on a regular basis. I regularly sit with children at evening services and worship with them.

These children do this from faith and from a strong relationship with God. To hear the conviction from the mouths of children is to hear the way that I imagine the disciples spoke of Jesus when he walked with them. Theirs is a faith uncomplicated by cynicism and maturity. They feel God and they know God. Their celebration is real and their commitment to their Church comes from believing it is a good place to be. Their willingness to learn about the word of God rivals most of the adults in Church. Our children have much to teach us all about faith, and now is the time to start learning.

I started by asserting that the Church of Scotland has a unique, strong, and impressive history and also that there are the signs that give the indications of a bright future in children's ministry. I believe that this is something we can be proud of, something that should celebrate in the ongoing life and growth of God's community here in Scotland. This insider does not hold that pride is a sin: I believe that we must recognise the great treasure God has given us in our children, and that we are responsible for enabling their ministries and sharing in the coming Kingdom with all children.

Children First? You bet!

Nine:

A COOL KIRK? INSINUATING YOUNG PEOPLE INTO THE CHURCH:

i) ECUMENICAL ADVENTURES

Chris Docherty

Chris Docherty has been the Youth Officer for the Archdiocese of Glasgow since 1995. He has been involved in the Church of Scotland National Youth Assembly since 2000, as well as a variety of other ecumenical adventures through ACTS. He lives in the Catholic Worker community in Glasgow, a house of hospitality for people seeking asylum in Britain.

A Catholic insider?

My points of connection and crossover with the Church of Scotland have been largely at a national level on youth ministry projects. What follows, then, is largely a series of narratives about my encounters with the people and practices of the Church of Scotland over the years, with some points of reflection about what this might be saying about the inside of the Kirk. I have chosen not to go down the line of providing an analysis of statistics of Church attendance, because it seems to me that what is central to discussions about the Church and young people is not 'are our worship buildings the right size?' but rather, 'are we being faithful to the mission Christ gave us, given the signs of the times that we are currently living through?'

My first awareness of Protestants came about when I was being prepared for my first term in primary school. The school badge for the local RC primary was round and featured a bright red cross in honour of St. Helen, the school patron. The local non-denominational Woodhill Primary, had a wee forest on it. I preferred the Woodhill badge and was a bit confused as to why I couldn't get one. Time went by and I got used to being a St. Helen's pupil and just thought that Woodhill Primary school was exactly the same as ours, with mass, prayers, a priest chaplain, preparation for the Sacraments, just with a nicer badge.

Woodhill Primary was at the end of our street and had a great big sloping grass field, which was ideal for playing football after school, and throughout the summers I and my pals (i.e. just the boys I knew best from school and church) would play against 'The Prods', or play mixed teams, or do other stuff that wee guys are wont to do. Our different church affiliation was seldom a big deal and never a source of animosity. When we did talk about it, it was a source of bemusement to us that being 'Protestant' didn't quite seem to mean as much to the other lads as being 'Catholic' did to us. Few of them went to church and only one or two were in the BB. At Eastertime, they used to wait for us while we ran from the field to the Good Friday services, then back to the field again after Stations of the Cross. It was all very strange. The point I'm making is that although we were aware of differences between us at this early age, they weren't so strong as to get in the way of our daily routine of being together, of spending time and sharing community.

Jubilee partnership

Pope John Paul II called for the Jubilee of the Year 2000 to be an intensely prayerful experience of reconciliation and justice-making amongst all people. As a response to this call, the Secretariat for Young People of the Catholic Bishops' Conference of Scotland invited the Church of Scotland to send some youth delegates to the World Youth Day being organised for August 2000 in Rome. To the surprise of many, the invitation was accepted with great enthusiasm. Not only that, but a reciprocal invitation was issued for some of the Catholic Diocesan Youth Workers and the Catholic development agency SCIAF to contribute a workshop to the 2000 Youth Assembly. I will focus on each of these events in turn.

The World Youth Day

The World Youth Days - the invention of Pope John Paul II - are vast celebrations for young people between the ages of 16 and 35. Over the last 16 years they have been in Rome, Buenos Aires, Manila, Santiago de Compostela, Denver, Paris, Czestochowa and Toronto. Anywhere between 1 and 5 million people converge on the city for a week, hosted by families, local churches, schools, supermarkets, campsites, in fact anywhere flat and dry where you can throw a sleeping bag! The pilgrims follow a programme of prayer, encounter, discussion, festival and liturgy, culminating in an overnight Prayer Vigil and Celebration of Eucharist with the Pope. It is fair to say that it is not an ecumenical event in design, but in almost every other dimension the WYD is an extraordinarily diverse global phenomenon. For the Jubilee Year of 2000, it was to take place in Rome, the boilerhouse of Catholicism.

Our preparation meetings began in the early months of 2000. Twenty Kirk delegates (most of whom I knew from my adventure at Youth Assembly) joined 100 young people from the Archdiocese of Glasgow for a series of monthly meetings around the city. Now, the World Youth Days can be profoundly stimulating, but also traumatic for any

Scots Catholic who takes part; not least because Catholics from other countries are much less self-conscious than we are about their faith. There is a joy and a generosity of spirit that faith brings to their sense of identity which, in ourselves, is usually attached to being gallus Glaswegians or feisty Scots. If the World Youth Day can be a challenge to a Scottish Roman Catholic even though the signs and symbols of Catholicism are the same across the world, what must it be like for a young Scots Presbyterian?

As leaders of the experience, we needed to reflect much more deeply about what God was inviting us into. The presence of what we might be tempted to call 'others' always reminds us of the diversity that already exists amongst the Catholic young people. We were not adding one homogeneous lump of Protestants to a larger homogeneous lump of Catholics. It raised all the thorny issues about Eucharist, authority, belonging, faith, difference, Scripture, ministry and approaches to worship. What changes, however is the context of the dialogue. Our young people meet at the initial meetings and take part in varying icebreakers with various amounts of dread. So the first thing they might learn about someone is that they too come from Clydebank, or that they too are a closet S Club 7 fan. They have fun, they connect, they are glad to know someone - and then it dawns on them that one of them is Catholic, the other Presbyterian. But they can't go back and redefine their experience in light of this new and possibly ominous information. So now they are two pals exploring their differences and their connections together. They are committed to preserving the friendship wherever that conversation might go, because they realise that in their 'difference' they have something to offer one another.

From a certain point of view, the World Youth Day is a global Youth Assembly, with the high standard of audio-visual work, keynote speakers from around the world and the vibrant music ministry. However, as an experience on the ground WYD is a pretty ramshackle affair. The key metaphor of 'pilgrimage' is taken quite directly. We travel light, there's a lot of walking, waiting in food queues and trailing across the public transport system (when it works), singing Scottish anthems! We sleep on the floor in schools where the showers are warm if you're lucky, and inside if you're luckier. At least one night is spent sleeping in fields with millions of people, in hail, rain or shine. It's a difficult experience for Catholics and Catholic Youth Officers. We have realised that an element of trust, faith and surrender is required. The participation of the Church of Scotland in the World Youth Days has added a great depth to the pilgrimage for all of us. As a planning team we were very mindful of this, and worked closely with Church of Scotland staff, to work out the most effective way of preparing the group for the journey. At our planning meetings, we integrated the small reflection groups; young Presbyterians contributed to the music ministry, and the reading of prayers; and the CofS team facilitated one of the plenary planning meetings in the St. Mungo Museum of Religious Life and Art. When the time came to celebrate a final mass before leaving, we ran a special session to look at the issue of liturgy, ministry and eucharist. We reassured everyone not to worry about the standing up, sitting down and the various responses, but invited them to join prayerfully in the experience of the local faith community. The response was very positive, and we were pleased that many aspects of the liturgy were accessible and spoke to everyone.

On one day in Rome, we were to visit St. Peter's basilica. As we trooped up the Via Della Conciliazione, I was trying to explain to the Kirk group about my ambivalence towards the symbolism of the Vatican, that it represented both a wonderful tradition and the scandal of Authoritarianism to me. I was a little crestfallen and confused when one responded, 'but it's really lovely!' They just don't get it sometimes, these Protestants, I thought.

During the pilgrimage to Rome, our group was invited to contribute to a Jubilee Radio programme and so we sent people from both RC and CofS to go along and share their impressions. For the most recent event in Toronto 2002, the Very Rev John Millar, former Moderator, addressed the pilgrimage group as part of an ecumenical Taizé prayer in the St. Andrew's RC Cathedral in Glasgow. As I said to him myself on the day, my granny wouldn't have believed it. The following month the Most Rev Mario Conti, the new Archbishop of Glasgow addressed the group on the day he had received the pallium (a length of cloth, symbolising his ministry as archbishop) from the Pope. In these two encounters it seemed to me that young Christian people are keen and willing to engage in conversations with church leaders as witnesses to the gospel, not just as institutional managers. The Former Moderator and the Archbishop, for their part, relished the opportunity to listen and to laugh and to share their own faith convictions with our merry band of pilgrims. It is sadly predictable however, that our collaborations have been condemned by Catholic 'traditionalists' on the one hand and the Orange Lodge on the other.

A further development between the experiences in Rome and Toronto was that Steve Mallon, the CofS's National Youth Adviser, was able to involve the local Canadian Presbyterian community in Toronto as hosts during our pilgrimage. To my regret, they had not already been approached by the local World Youth Day organisers and were delighted to host some visitors from Scotland. When the local governor found out about this oversight, they were given VIP tickets to some of the major celebrations. I hope that next time it will be unremarkable that different Christians attend the World Youth Day. Each day we took part in discussion groups facilitated by different bishops and cardinals. During question and answer sessions, our faithful Kirk reps contributed with energy, and with insight, no doubt tapping into debate fever from the Youth Assembly! Each time they said who they were and where they came from, there was rapturous applause from all the other delegates. What delighted me in Toronto however, was that the Kirk delegates raised general questions and issues about faith. Ecumenical discussions don't always have to be about ecumenism, and I look forward to seeing how we can build this model of 'churches together' in Scotland. In this way our partnership, which began in Glasgow, continues to cause ripples beyond our own national boundaries.

For their part the Kirk delegates talk about experiencing the global church in a way that Presbyterianism alone cannot provide for them. It is a truly Biblical experience, in the tradition of the perilous Exodus, to stand amongst 2 million young people waving enough flags to begin a riot in most situations, coming together to praise God and celebrate their diverse unity. I hope that this is what 'catholic' is meant to be. Our sensitivity to liturgy, silence, drama, movement and ritual is appreciated as a complement to the living out of the Word. The age-old adage that we have more in common than what separates us, becomes very apparent in these situations.

National Youth Assembly

I was in awe of the logistical majesty of my first experience of Youth Assembly, which took place in Heriot Watt University in April 2000. 'How do they manage to pull this off? How do they get so many non-youth ministry people to come along for four days and pour all this effort into the youth?'

The theme was 'Water', and for some reason we were approached to do a workshop on the Seven Deadly Sins. I was impressed with the scriptural and theological passion of the delegates. There was a range of viewpoints; from fiery fundamentalisms, to the broad band of the confused that want to love God and follow Jesus in an increasingly hostile and stressful world. It was quite amusing to take questions about being Catholic. It was like a sci-fi movie where inquisitive scientists turn to the life-form emerging from the flying saucer and bashfully say 'So what is life like on your planet?' All in all, there was a pretty jovial atmosphere, with lots of jokes floating around about Catholics and Protestants, none of it negative, hostile or 'sectarian' in any way.

I was amazed at the other aspects of Presbyterian life in the Youth Assembly. Talking plays a big part. The debate culture is deeply and fervently cherished, with young people (of varying levels of clarity and confidence) getting the opportunity to make their point. From an 'outside' perspective this was amazing. I tried, but could not imagine the same forthright discussion taking place between the 8 bishops of Scotland and 400 young Catholics. It would not have had the same feeling of mutual accountability somehow. The workshop and worship options also covered a broader range than I had seen before. At a Catholic event, there may be inputs/workshops on favourites like Justice and Peace, Pro-Life Issues, Music, Scripture and so on, followed by a celebration of mass. At Youth Assembly there was a space dedicated to young people and sexuality, a dream room, a comedy slot, keynote speakers, night-club worship, gospel choirs, movie workshops, storytellers...There seems to be more scope for experimentation and creativity within the centralised structures of the Kirk. Ironically, Catholicism is quite devolved in its deployment of youth ministry resources by comparison. This makes it difficult for us to hold a national event on a par with Youth Assembly. There is much greater emphasis placed on formal Catholic Education in schools compared to informal education. The semi-parliamentary nature of Assemblies in the Presbyterian tradition gives the Youth version a higher profile. It seems that if there's to be a debate and a vote to be had, local churches will tend to be keen to send representatives. In Catholicism, our preference is to support regional events where they can be demonstrated to provide ongoing benefit to local parish life.

There is a commitment amongst the young people and the Youth Work staff to examine the really difficult issues about pluralism, difference, authority and change. A space is created in which the institution stretches itself, almost to bursting point to say 'ok, we all disagree about this, but our commitment to explore the disagreement together is one of the marks of the followers of Christ'. I would cite the presence of various Conveners of Boards, project managers, elders, clerks and moderators as evidence that young Presbyterians are being taken more and more seriously by the whole Kirk.

At subsequent Youth Assemblies, we have contributed workshops on the Stations of the Cross, and the theme of 'No Escape'. There has been a subtle shift away from the Catholics only talking about "Catholic stuff", but still bringing reflections and experiences from within the broad tradition of Catholicism. The theme this year is to be 'Labyrinth': a rich and textured word that raises issues on levels other than denominational differences. Could the future of Scottish Christian Youth ministry lie with more interdependent joint-mission projects like this?

Last thoughts

All is not uniformly joyful and rosy. On a recent pilgrimage to the ecumenical monastic community of Taizé, one Church of Scotland woman from the Highlands felt that with its monks, icons and candles, 'it's a bit too Catholic'. This would be news to the monks, who have been drawn from a wide variety of Orthodox, Reformed and Catholic traditions. Does this just reflect one woman's particular Highland upbringing, or is it about the apparent bipolarity of Scottish Christianity - that things are either Roman Catholic or Presbyterian? For her, faith and worship had to look like a small group of people talking about Scripture, trading quotations. A generation ago, Catholics would have felt equally uneasy about sitting sharing reactions to a passage from the Bible. Only 'non-Catholics' do that, you know? Places like Taizé and, closer to home, Iona, and the work of evangelical youth ministry organisations remind us of the larger world and broader faith family that we belong to, in which we are called to be mature participants. Current global concerns about justice, trade, war and peace call us back to our apostolic origins as peacemakers. We will rediscover our unity, the unity that Jesus prayed for, in our common mission of announcing the reign of God amongst all peoples.

The Kirk that I know has a real future and a vital contribution to make to Scotland. Like other Christian communities, it is experiencing a certain diminishment from the heydays of the previous centuries, but the youth work that is going on is not trying to rebuild that past, preferring to discover God's new dream for his people. All 'youth ministers' face a tension between enabling individuals to undergo a personal conversion to faith (which we can do quite well) and enabling that conversion to bear fruit within the messy matrix of a local diverse faith community (which we find quite difficult). II is creative and generous in its involvement of young people and its invitation to other Christians to be a part of the journey. It is intelligent and capable of critical self-reflection and willing to go beyond its own boundaries and structures in order to hear a new word from God. The church is dying, but it is also living. It's a Jesus thing.

Perhaps in a 'church without walls', there is no outside?

ii) ASKING QUESTIONS, FINDING ANSWERS

Steve Mallon

Steve Mallon is the Church of Scotland's National Youth Adviser. With over 20 years experience in working with young people, Steve has been at the forefront of youth initiatives, education and training since joining the Board of Parish Education in 1992. Steve has both a BA in Commerce and an Msc in Applied Social Sciences and is currently working towards completion of a doctorate in Education at the University of Strathclyde.

We must not cease from exploration and the end of all our exploring will be to arrive where we began and to know the place for the first time.
T S Elliot

Tonight I spent the evening with a group of young adults, all of them connected to the church and involved in my work in one way or another. Their ages range from nineteen through to twenty-seven. Their backgrounds vary as do their gender, sexuality and employment status. Many of them are at university and some are unemployed, some of them know what they want to do with their lives but many of them haven't a clue. Some of them express faith in very evangelical terms, others in much more liberal ways. They are all different. But the amazing thing about this group, the one thing that sets them apart from their peers, is that they are all still in a conversation with the Church.

In the last 20 years or so - probably longer - the number of young people attending churches in the UK has dropped considerably. This is a matter of record and is something that is easily proven. But we don't need any proof, do we? We have eyes and we have seen the exodus. We have felt the pain and confusion as our sons and daughters, our friends, our grandchildren have arrived at a point in their lives where they have made the decision that they can no longer journey with the Church. And so they have left.

This is the present reality of life in the Church of Scotland. Its history with young people is not good, and that history has paralysed many of us from doing anything to change it. And yet in the middle of all of that misery, God is doing a new thing. It has taken time; it is still in its infancy, but it is happening. In this chapter I want to make the case that gradually the Kirk is gaining confidence and, more importantly, gaining ground. We are winning young people back.

I began working for the Church of Scotland 10 years ago. I succeeded the late Graham Aitken as the Youth Adviser to the Presbytery of Glasgow. I began the new job full of faith, enthusiasm - and terror! What would it be like? What on earth was I going to do? Why in God's name had I left a secure job for this? One of the first things that hit me was a statement my predecessor had made in his last report to the Presbytery. He said that 'youth work was not in decline but in its terminal stages'. People on hearing this sat up. Many brows were furrowed. Many hands were wrung. Many heads were scratched, and souls searched. What were we to do?

All that happened was that the problem got bigger and bigger; and so when I arrived in post full of my naïve enthusiasm and expectations of a Church that would joyfully sing, 'Shine Jesus Shine' together, what I found instead was a demoralised Kirk. One that had lost its way at least with regard to working with young people, and was scrambling around in the dark. Or maybe it wasn't so much that people were in the dark, perhaps in reality they were wearing blindfolds.

'Youth work in its terminal stages'... It's dead. It's too late. There's no point. There's nothing we can do. People simply didn't know what to do. How could this have happened? What do we do? Is there any hope?

The first thing we need to do in this type of discussion is to stop wringing our hands, and then concentrate on some truth. It can be easier to live with clichés these days, and the image of 'young people leaving the churches in the UK' is one such cliché. It's much more difficult to begin thinking about what we should do in the face of such a huge challenge. The first step in meeting this challenge is to have a realistic grasp of the context in which this has happened.

Young people and institutions

Over the last few decades young people have been disengaging from many institutions, not just the churches. For example in 1997, a poll suggested that 84% of young people in the UK thought that politicians didn't listen to young people's concerns[1]. Young people have been saying this for years and politicians have systematically ignored them. The result? A survey by MORI in 2000 suggested that only 40% of 18-24 year olds were registered to vote.[2] Trades Unions have struggled to win new recruits and have realised that they have an image problem.[3] A poll for Reader's Digest Magazine, also carried out by MORI, suggested that 52% of young people aged 15-25 think that there will no longer be a monarchy in the UK in 50 years' time, with a quarter of the poll suggesting it will have disappeared in just 10 years.[4]

We have to see that there has been a general trend towards disengagement from institutions on the part of young people over the last 20 or so years, and the Church has been affected by that trend as much as the other institutions mentioned. Many institutions have been slow to recognise this trend and even slower in trying to do something about it. The Scottish Parliament's Local Government Committee recently recommended that young people should be able to vote in council elections from the age of 16 and should be allowed to become councillors from the age of 18. This would get young people involved in the democratic processes at an earlier age, in the hope that their interest might be encouraged and sustained. Trades Unions are trying to deal with their image problem and to recruit younger members in association with the National Union of Students, to make the transition from study to work also a transition from one union to another. The monarchy's best hope with young people will be to show Princes William and Harry living as contemporary lives as is possible. The future of the British monarchy may depend on this.

No such thing as society

These words are attributed to Margaret Thatcher. For many people they will forever epitomise her administration as Prime Minister of the UK. The young people we live with now are in that sense her product, her progeny. They do not espouse the language of society, but the language of rampant individualism: what's in it for me? We cannot blame them. They were fed such an attitude along with their daily bread - this is how things were and how things were presented to them at this time in our history. Many of them have absorbed it now and it's part of their genetic make up. The problem for the church - and to a similar extent for the other institutions mentioned above - is that the church can only work within a community-based model. The gospel of Jesus Christ is about good news for the world; it's not just good news for you. The gospel of Jesus

---

[1] http://news.bbc.co.uk/1/hi/uk/politics/38126.stm 9 December 1997
[2] 'The Big Turn Off', MORI and Adam Smith Institute, 2000
[3] 'Reaching the Missing Millions', TUC, 2001
[4] Reader's Digest, September 2001

Christ challenges every statement that starts with 'I' or 'me' and instead asks for it to be rephrased to use 'we' and 'us'. The problem is, that ain't how young people have been brought up: and so there now exists a culture gap between the church and young people which is not so much about the clothes we wear, or our choices of music - if only it were that simple. Instead this culture gap is about the way that we choose to be together.

Many of the young people who have been involved in the church until late adolescence will leave because they just can't understand what the church culture is all about. Many will move from one church to another until they find one that will scratch their own individual itch. All of this means that the church continues to be denuded of its youth and its strong limbs - or some of them, anyway - and therefore the potential for paralysis continues.

While this culture gap undoubtedly exists, that does not mean that it cannot be bridged. It is the responsibility of the Kirk to build that bridge, to invade the land of rampant individualism and to tell a new story to its inhabitants. To woo the generation of young people who have been taught to put themselves at the centre of everything, with the gospel of Christ that teaches us to lose ourselves for the sake of the Kingdom of God.

The credibility gap

The other problem we have is that the world has moved on in so many directions and the church has just put down roots and stayed put. The church was never meant to be settled. It was meant to be an ever-evolving organism. Always on the move, always ready to follow the pillar of fire. Always waiting for the still small voice to whisper a new destination or stage in the journey. Instead the Kirk has become stuck. It is hampered by its own sense of its history and what it feels it is supposed to be in our national life, instead of accepting what it is. And the reasons for this are clear. When everything else in life has been changing rapidly, the Kirk has been the one place to stand still and so for some is the only safe place left. Many of us will recognise this.

There is a credibility gap. Much of what we say and how we say it doesn't seem to be credible; and to a cynical and individualist younger generation it may not even make sense.

A shifting paradigm

There are two ways we need to move forward. One is in the way that we look at young people, and the other is in how we work with them. I think both of these things are changing. I can say that as a statement of hope, but I can also back it up with stories from around Scotland and my direct experience of working with young people.

Recently I was doing some work in Belfast, which involved giving a 'lecture' - to a very small audience. One of the issues we discussed - the small audience and I - was the way we tend to view young people. Aristotle is quoted as having said, 'when I consider the younger generation I despair for the future of civilisation!' in c. 300 BC. I think adults have been in despair at the prospect ever since.

In preparation for my lecture in Belfast I did a web search of the BBC News website. I simply entered the words 'youth in Belfast' and the following were the top 10 results:

Youth critical after road crash

Youth on terrorist charges

Paint attack 'was paramilitary'

Youth remanded on stab charges

Police to close Belfast pub

Scheme targets disaffected youth

Ulster youth group gets Lawrence award

Youth faces car abduction charges

Child taken in stolen car

Youth charged after serious assault

As a list, it makes depressing reading: only one positive story. And there's the rub. This is part of the natural order of things. The older generations sometimes need to feel that the younger generation is making a mess of things. It's the way it has always been for some folk. It's how we tend to validate ourselves and how we mitigate our jealousy at no longer being young. But in doing it, we only serve to create a huge injustice; and instead of building a bridge to young people, we dismantle it and make it harder than ever for us to reach them and for many of them to hear our voices.

As Stephen Covey has said, 'the way we see the problem *is* the problem'.[5] If we always discuss young people within the context of 'problem' then we will never get past where we are today. We have to challenge our thinking. We have to begin to see what is good in the culture of young people - however different it is from our own. More importantly, we need to find ways of making sense to young people, of chiming with the things that keep them awake at night, of helping them realise their need to connect, to be part of a community, to give, to love.

The author Douglas Coupland puts this idea beautifully in his book, *Life After God*. He says 'Now - here is my secret: I tell it to you with the openness of heart that I doubt I shall ever achieve again, so I pray that you are in a quiet room as you hear these

[6] Stephen Covey, *Seven Habits of Highly Effective People,* Simon and Schuster, 1989

words. My secret is that I need God - that I am sick and can no longer make it alone. I need God to help me give, because I no longer seem to be capable of giving; to help me be kind, as I no longer seem capable of kindness; to help me love, as I seem beyond being able to love.'[6]

These are the words of a prophet from the younger generation. Telling us that he needs God. Telling us that he needs to relate, to love, to give, to be kind. Are we too busy complaining about young people to hear their cry for something authentic? Their cry for something that they can believe in and depend on? Their cry for something that will not spoil or fade?

The way we see the problem is the problem. If your views of young people are profoundly negative, then shame on you. If we want to see more young people in church, then it starts right here. We need to celebrate our young people, their achievements and also their mistakes. We need to embrace all of it.

I went through this kind of process with a couple of Kirk Sessions recently. Two churches in the process of joining together in a voluntary union wanted to discuss how they could make young people a higher priority in their lives as a new congregation. When I asked the elders to finish the statement 'young people are...' the results were profoundly negative. This was not unexpected and at least it was honest. The good thing is that by the end of our time together, that same group had a plan that would involve them talking to young people, listening to their views and then doing something positive about what they were going to hear.

The way we see the problem is the problem. If that's your problem, then it's time to change.

The way we work with young people

I am happy to report that there is an area of life in the Church of Scotland that has seen unprecedented growth in the last decade! Not long after I came into post we hosted a gathering for youth workers that were employed in a paid capacity by local congregations. All in all there were about 10 people in such positions at the time. Today there are around 100 and new ones are popping up all the time. This is good news and represents a significant shift in the way we are choosing to work with young people.

What difference does having a paid youth worker make? Let me tell you about 'Tony the Christian'. Tony Stephen is based in the Banchory churches project near Aberdeen and he's been there for a good number of years now. Tony is one of the most effective and professional youth workers I have ever met. He has done a remarkable job, alongside some visionary leaders and amazing and dedicated volunteers. If you talk to social workers, teachers, community education workers, the police in Banchory (as I have) - they all know what Tony is doing. They all know about the project sponsored by

[7] Douglas Coupland, *Life After God*, Pocket Books, 1997

the two churches.

The kids in the local school refer to Tony as 'Tony the Christian', they all know he's from the church. He gets to do classes and assemblies and he's someone that young people in the community know they can turn to if they have a problem. Christian youth work and youth workers are generally not highly regarded by professionals in other fields. This is not the case in Banchory where Tony and his team are seen as a vital part of the social mix for young people in the town. And the work that they do with kids in the churches is also growing. Young people are beginning to join the churches, get involved in what's going on, taking up challenges to work for charity projects at home and abroad. A success story.

This is a good story but it has to be borne in mind that in the Church of Scotland, the vast majority of our work with young people will always be done by volunteers. A church in the south side of the city of Glasgow decided to appoint a Youth Elder. In most churches such an elder would have a structural role. They might be 'in charge' of all the youth work or might co-ordinate all of the youth organisations. In this situation, the Youth Elder, Brenda, spent most of her time on the 'phone talking to the young people of the church and parish. She opened her home to them and they came in. She offered them sanctuary and they showed up. She offered them water from the well of Christ and they came to drink.

I once visited Brenda's house to interview a group of her young adults to ask for their views on the Church of Scotland. I came away with a quote that has haunted me ever since. They said that the Kirk was 'big, brown and boring'! And they were right! And yet, sitting in Brenda's house they looked anything but bored.

I lost contact with Brenda until recently, when I was delighted to hear that she was getting involved in youth work again after taking a wee rest. She will forgive me for saying that she is no spring chicken, but she is the real deal. She cares about young people. She wants them to know about God, to hear the old, old story in a way they can relate to and understand. The Kirk is full of people like Brenda and yet it acts as though it isn't. We don't seem to know how to celebrate our volunteers and what they give to us. We have to slay the dragon that says that only young people can do youth work and see that for the lie that it is. We need to affirm our mature volunteer force and encourage and enable them to do their job well. And these are all things that I see happening all over Scotland.

Times, they are a-changin'…

Ten years ago we were wringing our hands in despair. Ten years on we are singing a different tune. In May 2003, for the first time in its history, the General Assembly will receive a report from the National Youth Assembly. For the first time, young people in the church will have the chance to stand in the Assembly and tell the Ministers, Elders and other Commissioners what they have decided about key issues facing the Kirk today. For the first time, they will have elected their own to represent them in that Assembly. For the first time, they will answer questions for themselves. This is no mean feat for a Church that was in despair just 10 years ago.

The National Youth Assembly is one of the Kirk's foremost achievements in the last decade. It has enabled the institution to begin a different conversation with young people and amazingly young people have responded well. A few years into the process the Board of Practice and Procedure, having seen the success of the Youth Assembly, proposed that young people take part in the General Assembly from 1998. I did not think that this would work. I did not think that young people would want to spend a week in May with a bunch of what they might think of as "old fogies" ! I was so very wrong. In that first year, around 40 young people took part. The first voice heard in the first open debate was one of the young people. I sense a collective intake of breath as one of the Youth Delegates from the Presbytery of Aberdeen, Allan Millar, made history on that day.

Most recently is my own special story, where a group of young adults have emerged to get involved with me in the work we are doing together. Now our events are planned together. We meet monthly, we talk daily through internet forums, we email constantly. Their commitment amazes and humbles me. To still be in the Kirk in your 20s is surely a miracle in these days? Well, miracles are happening.

Inside Outside Verdict

This is all in stark contrast to the perspective about youth work Harry Reid has given us in his book. For reasons I can't fathom Harry has gone down the road of the doomsayers and given the impression that there is nothing positive to report about youth work in the church. As we have already considered, if you keep telling a person that they are rubbish at something, eventually they will prove you right. It is the same for the Kirk and its relationship with young people. The time has come for us to stop having these kinds of conversations and start talking about the places where good youth work is happening. And there are lots of them in the Kirk.

Harry asked Principal David Lyall of New College about what he thought might make young people return to the church. His answer? 'I simply don't have any answers.' When I first read this section of Harry's book I felt really sad because I work with the answers every day.

Today is the day for good news about young people in the Church of Scotland. This good news will encourage those who are still struggling to make things better as well as confirming the positive developments of those who have got out of the boat and started to walk on water. There is still a long way to go with many challenges ahead, but the journey out of despair has begun and there is no going back.

Ten:

REAWAKENING THE SPIRITUAL JOURNEY FOR ADULTS:

i) FAITH FOR LIFE: CRAFTING AN ADULT SPIRITUALITY

Fiona Fidgin

Fiona Fidgin is a Labyrinth facilitator and works for Altared Images, providing creative spiritual resources for church and community; she is also a member of the Iona Community. Fiona is a qualified primary teacher and worked as a youth and community worker with Mayfield Salisbury Church of Scotland in Edinburgh where her main emphasis was in running a neighbourhood flat for young people in the community.

I was on a train heading home when I found myself watching a group of lads getting ready to exit at the next stop. One of them had an interesting hoodie top. I couldn't make out the logo on the front of his top but as he turned around I smiled at the words on the back...'free thinkers are dangerous'.

Like most institutions, the church is not all that comfortable with free thinkers. It prefers the safety net of the status quo. It likes to know that there are clear, set boundaries, and rules and regulations that folk understand and abide by. Perhaps this is one of the reasons why the church is numerically in decline. It doesn't sit well with the post-modern agenda that positively encourages a free thinking mind of the pick-and-mix variety. Adults in the 21st century are looking for more from the church: women in positions of leadership, lay empowerment, relevant worship, equal dialogue - a chance to know that being a lay person matters and that they have something worthwhile and unique to contribute. The church has, on the whole, failed to nurture a lifelong faith development programme for its adults. It has assumed that the preaching of the word by the minister, and the occasional attendance at a lent group should be enough to sustain the faith of most adults. With so much emphasis on the importance of Sunday School and Bible Class, it is odd that the adults of the church have not had a similar learning programme. I secretly long for the day when the children stay in the church to do the 'real worship' and the adults go out to learn more about Jesus!

A Church of Scotland Board of National Mission report highlighted the fact that church membership is in decline, stating that If church congregations continue to fall at their current rate of 17,000 members a year, in 50 years' time there would be nobody attending services.[1] The Church would cease to exist. Fewer than 610,000 - 10% of the population - now belong to a Church congregation compared to almost three million Scots - 26% of the population - in 1930. The church is now in a fight for its own survival. Will Storrar from Edinburgh University points out that changes in society since 1950 mean that we can no longer expect people to support an institution - whether it be a political party, trade union or church - for life.[2]

If the church is going to continue, then some drastic learning needs to take place: learning for itself as a national body, learning for each of the parishes about their place in the community, learning for adults as they deepen their faith and understanding of God. In all of these, there needs to be an opportunity to grow and mature, a desire to develop, in the words of George MacLeod, 'new ways to touch the hearts of all', a chance to explore and question who we are and what we do, the ability to let go, to take new risks and push the boundaries. The church should not be afraid to do all of these things (and more!) and do it in an exciting, attractive, energetic, enthusiastic, passionate, exploratory and above all prayerful way that meets the needs of folk living in a post-modern 21st century society. This chapter seeks to explore the place of adults in the church. It looks at the current context and invites adults to reflect and evaluate on their faith and their life in the church; to explore ways of journeying the road together, teaching and learning from one another, to nurture an inclusive vision for continuous adult dialogue and growth; to nurture a faith for life. This is a job not just for those who work within the church at national level, it's not a job just for those who are ordained, it's not a job just for those who have responsibilities within the church - the challenge for change, for growth, for continuous learning is a job for the whole adult body of the church - a job for ALL.

The current context

What is happening to the church? Why are so many folk disinterested? Although attendance in churches is low and falling, 76% of the national population in 2000 admitted to spiritual and religious experiences.[3] Dr. David Hope, the Anglican Archbishop of York noted that large numbers of people say they pray, but they are not into organised religion. He urges for a more dynamic, flexible and responsive church.[4] And it hasn't been just the non-church folk that are staying away.

[1] *Report to the General Assembly* (2002), Board of National Mission. Reports to the General Assembly 2002, The Church of Scotland Board of Practice and Procedure.

[2] 'In Loving memory of the Church of Scotland', *Sunday Times* 21.4.02

[3] Hay, D. Hunt, K. (2000): *Understanding the Spirituality of people who don't go to Church*, University of Nottingham.

[4] Reid, H. (2002): *Outside Verdict: An Old Kirk in a new Scotland*, St. Andrew Press p.203

There's something interesting happening in the Christian community across the Western World. Very quietly and unobtrusively, one group of believers is growing on a daily basis. Who are they? They are the Christians who don't go to church any more. The ones who've given up altogether. Not the faith as such. Most still believe in Jesus, and struggle to live a life of discipleship. But they do it on their own, away from congregations and church structures.[5]

What is alarming in this context is that the church accepts no responsibility for the increasing tide of dissatisfaction, but continues to call into question the integrity of those who have been alienated.

The frustration with worship may be one of the reasons why folk have begun to leave the church - lay people are tired of being passive participants, being an audience to the minister. Harry Reid suggested that the church should exploit its preachers - and yet it seems that adults nowadays want more from worship than being preached at. Several frustrations have been noted:[6] a sense of boredom due to lack of connection and meaning; a feeling of isolation - not being able to understand the music and the language, feeling disconnected - the worship in church being unconnected in comparison to the secular 'holy' experience of special moments, at special times, with special folk. In short, little to stir the imagination or the senses, little use of symbols, rituals or actions that articulate something of the mystery of what it means to be human. The Very Rev Andrew McLellan, former Moderator of the Church of Scotland agrees that worship has been one of the factors in the church's decline, declaring that it has tolerated the second-rate and the second-best.[7]

Further dissatisfaction seems to lie in the politics of structure, power and control. The churches' understanding of ministry needs to be broadened, if lay people are to feel empowered. Becoming a youth worker is often the only road offered to adults who feel called to lay ministry. Presbytery structures seem reluctant to affirm ministry outside parish or beyond that of cleric. One hundred and forty women of the Kirk wrote a letter to the Board of Practice and Procedure expressing their disappointment at, again, a woman being turned down as Moderator. Folk are becoming increasingly angry at the sexism, hypocrisy, pretence, judgement and moralising which goes on in communities of Christians. It does not read well.

Enabling change

Some parishes, of course, do run good adult education courses, but the full potential of the parish as a community for ongoing religious and spiritual learning waits to be realised. Adults with a conscious desire to deepen their spiritual life are often viewed with suspicion rather than encouragement. The minister feels threatened, and other members of the congregation make the interested member feel awkward or rebellious.

5 Riddell, M. Pierson, M. Kirkpatrick, C. (2000) *The Prodigal Project: Journey into the emerging Church*, SPCK, p.1
6 Reid, H. (2002), *ibid.*
7 Reid, H. (2002), p.204

It's time for the adults of the church to be involved in the process of change. The church for too long has been interested in preserving the 'outer appearance': sustaining its buildings, the need for young people (to keep the church going), numbers, membership, control, prestige, power, appearance etc. - rather than looking towards the 'inner': sustaining its people, empowering, nurturing, feeding, nourishing, accepting, welcoming, giving away power - becoming vulnerable, developing a sense of community, movement, reflecting, listening. The former is about show, achievement and status; the latter requires adults to engage with their hearts and not their heads, to be passionate about living the Gospel, following Christ on the edge of an unstable rocky road. It's not safe and it's not secure, but it seems to me that the future of the church isn't either - so what is there to lose? I believe that as adults we need to start taking some responsibility for the development of our faith. For too long many of us have developed no further in our understanding of faith than when we were in Sunday school.

The demise of the Scottish Churches Open College reflects on the poor attitude of the churches of all denominations towards adult learning, and besides, the financial value they place on it. Our learning need not affirm merely the academic but include the intuitive, creative side to our humanity. For too long we have assumed that intellect was the primary avenue for experiencing the Divine, to nourishing the soul, and have ignored the imagination and other faculties of knowing mystery. I want to suggest, further, that it would do no harm for the church to reflect on whether, after 35 years, the ministry of women has made a difference. Historically, the feminine has been destroyed through centuries of patriarchal domination, through fear of creativity and the traits associated with the feminine - such as empathy, curiosity, community and holistic thinking. Women have brought a balance back enabling integration between the feminine and the masculine, between the receptive and the assertive, the imagination and the reason. We need to nurture this relationship, engaging in its free flowing pattern in order to discover a more holistic sense of ourselves as human beings made in the image of God.

The church needs to develop a new identity, one that provides spiritual guidance and nurtures creativity. There is a saying: 'Religion is for those who are scared to death of hell. Spirituality is for those who have been there!' We have often confused Religion with Spirituality, the container with the process, the liturgy and act of worship with the inward activity of awe and wonder. I want to question whether adults in the church have been enabled to become spiritually mature? To grow in an ever-deepening sense of compassion, lessening the fear of change and of the differences between us. The church needs to explore ways of offering spiritual nurturance within, as well as outside the religious service. Many seekers leave the church with disappointment, feeling a lack of spiritual nourishment and that the church is unable to help them with the transformations of their lives. Karen Armstrong, in the *History of God,* tells of her struggle as a nun to find God when she had no direct personal experience - how true is that for many of us? If the church is seen primarily as a place of spiritual maintenance it will be trying to hang on to its members. Little energy will be left for sharing the faith outside the community. If, on the other hand, the church is a place of encouraging spiritual growth and exploration, then folk will be attracted to it. We need to explore a variety of ways of engaging with the spiritual in a way that is outward-looking, catching imagination and curiosity: through seminars, debates, movies, the creative arts - processes that involve dialogue, reflection, awe, wonder, mystery. To complement this, we need to nurture a sense of the Divine in contemplation and prayer.

Worship and contemplation

We are dominated by the rush of life, 24 hours/7 days a week; our lives are out of balance, and we urgently need to re-address this. A church's worth is all too often seen in its busy, active community and social life, and if this is to be more than superficial, then there needs to be an adult base who are experienced in the contemplative dimension of both prayer and life. We are a generation who long for silence and yet are fearful of it. How does the church enable people to pray outside the context of a religious service? We need less petitioning to God and more ways to encourage a deep desire for a time of peace and quiet where that longing for a sense of the Divine is nurtured and quenched.

Worship and prayer should be central to the life of the church; and adults can play a huge part in this. The 'alternative worship' movement has been a soul-friend for folk who don't want to give up on their faith. Charlie Irvine, from Glasgow's 'Late, Late Service' and guitarist with 'Lies Damned Lies', comments that folk have gathered as a matter of survival. Not to prove a point, or to compete with more traditional patterns of worship, but rather to just try to function as people following Christ.[8] When Altared Images (the monthly contemporary worship based in the south side of Edinburgh) started in 1997, the intention was to enable worship for young folk, but it soon became evident that it was in fact the adults who were hungry and thirsty for a more inclusive, reflective approach to worship. The evening gatherings complemented the morning service by providing a contemporary approach to worship, where inclusive language, the use of space and arrangement of chairs, the inclusion of ritual and symbolic action, a time of dialogue, creativity or reflection and silence, were encouraged. A well thought-through theology of hospitality and worship enabled adults, from student age to pensioner, travelling from all over the central belt, to come and experience worship that connected with their life story, valued their questions, made little demands in terms of membership, and after three years, began to develop a sense of community and belonging.

[8] Riddell, M. Pierson, M. Kirkpatrick, C. (2000), p.14

There is a post-modern attitude that says folk don't want to join but they do want to belong. The church as a place of community may have an important part to play in the regeneration of the church. Many churches are actually too large for there to be much sense of community, and some adults find that the housegroup movement has been a soul-friend for them. The church, if adults are to grow in faith, should actively encourage the development of small groups where folk can come and explore issues of faith in a nurturing, caring, and supportive setting. Where the experience of letting go and vulnerability is not seen as unsafe and open to abuse, but is recognised as an honest encounter of who we are, our failing in the world and our need for healing, companionship, acceptance and growth. It is these sacramental moments that might articulate something of the 'Yes' to faith, the passionate heartfelt affirmation that knows we are loved - in spite of ourselves.

Ordinary situations - extraordinary possibilities

The *Church without Walls* report urged the church to explore new ways of being - and even now, after three years, we still hear the excuses: we can't do this overnight, it will take time. Nonsense! The church is being offered its own 'wake-up call', and still hesitates to take it. The journey into unfamiliar territory is scary and unpredictable, but with vision and a little courage, adults can begin a process of initiating how the church reaches out unconditionally to folk on the outside, and nurtures the faith development of those within it.

Exploring new possibilities of church was at the heart of a project known as 'Building Bridges of Hope' (BBH), an initiative of Churches together in Britain and Ireland (CTBI) and written in the book *Changing Churches* (Hinton 2002). BBH started as a three year ecumenical learning experiment where Christian communities agreed to create long-term commitment, to seek regular accompaniment, to welcome constructive criticism, to look at how the life of each of the churches might fit into the wider whole, and to seek God's presence in the world, not just in the church. At a time when the traditional church institutions were eroding, BBH was designed to see how Christians at the grassroots were responding to the challenge of change. From this first stage, seven key factors were identified to enable local Christian communities to engage in the mission of God in contemporary society. They were:

- **Focusing Vision.** The importance of local churches articulating their specific calling through integrated strategies for community engaging, mature spiritual life, enabling leadership and appropriate structure.

- **Building local partnerships.** The significance of seeking and forming partnerships of action with those of similar concerns in the wider community inside and outside the Church.

- **Sharing faith and values.** A commitment to exploring respectful and creative ways to share values, aspirations and faith, in and beyond church circles, in relation to the gospel story.

- **Nourishing daily living.** The critical need for believers old and new to relate biblical faith to personal life, work and culture in society today, through worship and reflection.

- **Developing shared leadership.** The importance of forming *in context* (clergy - lay and other forms of) team leadership, animated by one another and linked both to church learning institutions and to genuine community participation.

- **Becoming communities of learning.** Churches at every level need to become places where the lessons about how to be 'bridge builders' with others can be developed, consolidated and extended.

- **Willingness to be accompanied.** The value of welcoming systematic accompaniment and evaluation in non-directive ways beyond the local - and the networking of stories and experience in order to be able to look at each other with fresh eyes.

These learning indicators will be tested out in a wider, innovative context, including initiatives in dioceses, deaneries, provinces, ecumenical bodies, projects, action zones, experimental groups and training institutions: wherever the action is, or aims to be. The intention is that over a period of 2 - 5 years the results found will form a 'living laboratory' for the churches in Britain and Ireland concerning different, effective ways of doing Christian mission across a range of contexts and factors.[9]

   Many adults would die at the thought of being a 'living laboratory'; and yet in many ways, taking a good look at itself and encouraging an 'outside' accompanying person to do the same, would transform the life of many a parish. The notion of *praxis* (practice) is the fundamental staring point here. *Praxis* is the integration of action and reflection. Kathy Galloway, leader of the Iona Community reflects that this enables us to learn from our experience, to discover what it is that we need to nourish and sustain

[9] Hinton, J. (2002): *Changing Churches Building Bridges in Local Mission,* Churches Together in Britain and Ireland

our acting, and to identify and name that nourishment, whether it be song, prayer, silence, creativity, laughter, tears, the stories of a place, of people or whatever.[10]

The task ahead for adults, in the words of Kenneth White, is to 'select the features of real significance'. Is the church about numbers, membership, prestige and survival, or it is about relationship, passion, pain, nurture and spiritual growth? We need to hone as much energy into adult faith development as we do with our youngsters, or the church will soon be out of balance - if it isn't already. We need to do this not for the survival of the church, but rather to honour adults as spiritual beings, searching for a way that empowers them to serve the world in an active, self-aware and compassionate way, as people who bring with them unique hopes, dreams, history and longings of the soul. In our hearts we already know the features of real significance that are the tools for transformation... we need to start using them.

ii) THE EMPEROR'S NEW CHURCH?...

Stewart Cutler

Spending his teenage years in a Manse gave **Stewart Cutler** *an inside view of the ups and downs of church life. Despite this experience, he went on to study Community Education, paying his way through university by DJ-ing in clubs and pubs, before working after his graduation for several years as a youth worker in Carluke. His work since then has included training youth workers, developing Crossover Youth Festival, helping congregations to identify their priorities and plan their development, and producing resources for youth work and adult study groups. He is currently National Adviser in Adult Education with the Church of Scotland: encouraging grown-ups to keep learning about themselves, their world and God.*

This isn't working! There, I've said it. I feel better already. I've been meaning to say it for a long time - in fact I can't remember a time in the last 30 years when I haven't thought it. Oh - it's the Church I'm talking about, by the way.

I can't help feeling that we have become like the participants in the story of the Emperor's New Clothes. You know the story. The Emperor gets a new suit; he is actually naked but all his subjects are too scared to say it. Everyone knows. Everyone can see it, but it takes a little boy who doesn't know any better to break the ice. The Emperor is parading down the road with the crowds cheering, but as the Emperor passes, turning to their neighbour to whisper 'He's naked! Do you think he knows? Is he mad?' The

[10] Galloway, K. (2002): 'Camas - a faith reflection' (Unpublished).

little boy just says what he sees. He names the problem. Why did it take a child? The grown-ups all noticed. Were they scared to say? Fearful of the consequences? As I have travelled the country for the past six years talking to Kirk Sessions, Guilds, committees, young people, old people, ministers, youth workers, all of them people like you, most have recognised this very basic and obvious statement. This is not working. There is something very wrong with what the Church has become. The problem is it is not as obvious as the Emperor's problem. All he had to do was get dressed and get over the embarrassment. We have to start over again. Not tinker about with what we already have. We need to radically rethink how we 'do' church.

Promises, promises

I recently read the membership vows I made when I joined the Church of Scotland. I was immediately struck by the enormity of what I promised and confessed that day. I said out loud that I believed in God, Jesus and the Holy Spirit, and yet I have spent the past ten years trying to understand what that means. Some days I believe more than others. Some days I'm pretty certain that God exists and that He loves me. Some days I can't imagine that there is a God. I know I'm not alone in this. I know we all doubt, struggle and rejoice. We just don't talk much about it, especially in church.

I promised to give my time, talents and money: and I work for the church, so I do that all day, but how can I do that when I go home? What can I do if I don't want to teach Sunday School or Bible Class? How much money should I give? Who to? My church? Charities? Beggars on the street?

I promised to read my Bible regularly and pray. Has anyone else noticed that the Bible is actually quite hard to understand? And just how do you pray? What should you say? Is it OK to ask God for daft things? Do I need to use any particular words and talk in a different voice, like some ministers do? I promised to join regularly with fellow believers to worship on the Lord's day. But I have a range of excuses for not going to church often. For instance, I have two small kids: the youngest has his morning nap at 10.30am and lunch at 12. And if we ever want to visit our parents, we have to go at the weekend because they live so far away. Even when I do drag myself along I find what we do together all too often anything but worshipful. I find myself becoming angry because I know what it *can* be like. A standard Sunday service, and even a nice fluffy evening service with more modern music, just doesn't relate to the rest of my life. It's not that I don't have a long attention span, or that I don't like old hymns. I do. I enjoy listening to people discuss theology, life and stuff. Maybe the key is that I like to be able to talk back?

I have experienced God in worship, but rarely on an average Sunday. You know that feeling when you just know that God is in the room? It mostly happens when I've shared time with people; got to know them a bit; heard all their best jokes and some of their bad ones; found out what makes them tick and then thanked God for the time we have spent together. In other words, it happens when worship reflects the life of the community.

But you can't do that for 200 people: I know that's what you're thinking. And yet you are also probably remembering your own experiences of closeness to God, and they are probably not unlike mine. That's the heart of the problem. I have felt close to God standing in a field in the rain with 10,000 other people. I didn't even know many of them, but we had shared a space in time; four days journeying together. It *is* true! Size *doesn't* matter! We will never have a sense of belonging and community if a lot of us only ever spend an hour a week together, mostly looking at the back of each other's heads. How can we get to know each other? Share our hopes and dreams and doubts and questions? Be a caring and compassionate group of people who go the extra mile for each other and for the people we are supposed to care for in our communities?

Think about what you would have to do in your church to help every member get involved in one act of service (the helping people kind of service) to the wider community in a year. Just stop and consider how your church could make that happen. Now think of the difference it might make to your church and your community if you actually made it happen. Think of all the people you would help. Think of the things you could accomplish with, say, two hundred people each giving up a day to work for other people. Think of the skills that the people in your congregation have but never get the chance to use. Imagine what could happen.

What could you to do to help everyone in your church read the Bible, just once a week, and actually have the chance to talk to others about what it means to them? To find out about what was going on when that passage was written, who wrote it, and who were they writing to. How it connects to other passages and previous and future events. The Bible is a simple yet complex book. It can speak to us when we just pick it up, open it and read. It somehow connects to who we are and our needs at that time. How much more does it say when we take time to discover where it came from? Why it exists; the people whose journey it chronicles; how Jesus spoke to the culture of his time and to our culture today.

DO something! Anything!...

The Church of Scotland seems to have run out of things to say, or at least ways to say things in a manner that people will pay attention to and engage with. What is the Church saying about war? About poverty? About HIV / Aids? About famine? It sometimes seems that the only thing we ever talk about is sex. It is an important issue, and deserves our attention, but so are all the others. We have become fearful of causing offence when I'm sure people would much rather the Church said something definite, even if it was for them to argue with. The Church played a central role in the creation of the Scottish parliament. We have good people working in the Church and Nation Committee looking at political issues. Unfortunately we also seem to have signed up to the old (false) adage that religion and politics don't mix in our personal and congregational lives. Maybe we assume that everyone knows what we think. Maybe we don't know what we think. How much do we reflect on our faith, for instance, when we come to vote? Do we let our elected representatives know how we feel about issues? Or have we succumbed to the apathy that has swept our nation? It is part of our duty, both as citizens and as Christians to make sure that our politicians do their best to help the disadvantaged and the vulnerable. That means voting, campaigning and participating in politics at every level.

This apathy and lack of debate and discussion has affected almost every area of the church. In my most cynical moments I wonder if the church even knows why it exists. I'm sure that the vast majority of our members have no idea what being a 'Presbyterian' means. 'Why have Presbyteries at all?' Isn't it interesting that some of the reactions to the consultation on how best to organise what is essentially our management system, have thrown up that response? Those of us (un)lucky enough to have attended Presbytery meetings with any kind of regularity may very well agree with the sentiment, but it must go deeper than this reactionary response.

So, why have Presbyteries at all? Mostly because that's what Presbyterians do! I think we really lack a sense of belonging to our church. I'm not sure how connected people feel even to the other people in their congregation, never mind the whole Church of Scotland. Sometimes it seems that people get more worked up about moving the furniture in their church building than about visiting the sick. How do we get to a place where people notice who attends worship - not to gossip about what they might be up to if they are not there, but out of concern for what might be wrong with them, and a willingness to help? One of the most disappointing things I have ever seen is a sign on a local church that offers 'tea, coffee and "friendship"'. Note - "friendship" in inverted commas. Why "friendship"? Does that mean that the tea and coffee are real and the "friendship" isn't? Maybe they are actually being honest. Is "friendship" what we offer? A veneer of sincerity and caring, but no real depth?

Why do we send children to Sunday School and bible class? 'To learn more about God and discuss and share that learning with each other' - that would be the obvious answer. Why do we stop doing this when we become grown-ups? One of the most interesting experiences I have ever had was a group of people who met after the Mission Scotland campaign ten or so years ago. I was eighteen at the time and I was asked to co-lead a group that would explore the basics of Christianity. I said yes, and on the first night a whole range of people turned up. Among them were new Christians who had gone forward at the Billy Graham events and some people from the church who had 'rededicated' themselves, including the Session Clerk. We talked and shared together for ten weeks, and in that period discovered that the Session Clerk (aged 72) had never had this kind of opportunity to talk about his faith since he left Bible Class fifty-five years earlier.

As more people grow up with no reference to the church, surely our Adult Education has taken on a new importance, not only in the way that we explain a foreign concept like church, but how we nurture people within our fellowships. We can no longer claim to be anything but a struggling minority in today's society. The sooner we realise that the majority of the population of Scotland don't actually attend church, apart from weddings and funerals, the better - because until we recognise this, we will continue to assume people understand what we are talking about and we can continue to pretend that we understand too.

Try this exercise: explain 'salvation' without using any other Christian words. It's a word we use every week, maybe even every day - and yet I would guess that you had to think hard, firstly about what it means, and then to translate it from Christian-ese into ordinary language. We will only be able to reach out to people and have meaningful discussions about faith when we can talk about it in a language that is understood by all. And that means talking in the language of feelings! People experience God. One of my most powerful experiences of God was at a U2 concert. God was in the room. So was half the Celtic team, but that's another story. U2 have managed to write about faith in a language people understand. Their music embraces questions and doubts and hopes and fears and yet people question their commitment to Jesus because they don't come on stage preaching. I wonder how may albums even the best overtly Christian artists sell, and who makes people - those with some, little or no faith - think most?

So why not "just do it"?

The Church belongs to everyone. To you and to me. Over the two thousand years since Jesus walked among us, we seem to have recreated much of what He appears to have been most against. When Jesus died on the cross, the veil of the inner temple was torn in two. It signified that there were to be no barriers between us and God. We have rules that mean only ministers can conduct communion. Can anyone explain that to me? Why can't I do it? At which point did Jesus stop during the last supper and say 'when you do this remember me, but only if you have a guy (or since the 1970s, maybe even a woman), who went to University for years, passed selection school and has been called by a congregation and approved by Presbytery, in the room.'

And what about the conduct of worship? Is the minister the only one with an opinion? Why can't I hear from you? Get to hear how you became a Christian. Find out what you think and what you struggle with. Pray for you. Have you pray for me. Have you ever wondered at the point in communion when we are invited to share 'the peace' why we all get all shy and embarrassed? It's because we don't feel any sense of connection to the people around us. We are uncomfortable with displays of emotion. Even shaking hands can be too much for us. We dread the extrovert who has the gumption to actually hug people and, heaven forbid, maybe even kiss them, heading our way!

It all seems so far away from the seemingly simple, yet effective early years of the church. People believed in Jesus. They shared their lives together, their possessions, their skills, their food, their worship. Yes, the churches had leaders, but the rest of the fellowship didn't abdicate all their responsibilities for pastoral care, worship and administration to those poor souls. They played their part: took their turn; asked their questions; shared their thoughts.

I was struck by the simplicity and bravery of this posting on an internet forum:

> Are house groups too basic a concept? There has been huge spiritual growth within our church since they took off in a big way. Visitors are very quickly invited to existing groups. "Seekers" and new Christians have new groups created for them...

The simple bit is the use of house groups. People meeting to talk and share. You're probably thinking, 'I couldn't do that. They would all know more than me. I'd be scared. I don't have time.' So is everyone else. Swallow hard (that's your pride you feel sliding down), and get on with it. The brave bit is asking the people in the community what they think about the church. They might actually tell us. I'm not sure we are ready for that. Are you?

So, I think we can all agree that the church we have is broken. It doesn't work the way it can and should. So what can we do? Well, we can start by taking back our church. Stop giving power to others and supporting the system that has got us in this mess. The church will only change if you change it. No one can make it better for you. I realised a long time ago that it is easy to criticise the church from the outside. It is easy to highlight the faults. It is much harder to struggle from the inside. Harder to work for change and progress. And if you are thinking that you are OK and you can manage, and that it will be all right, reflect on these words:

It is always far easier to have faith in your own goodness than to confront others and fight for your rights. It is always easier to hear an insult and not to retaliate than have the courage to fight back against someone stronger than yourself; we can always say we're not hurt by the stones others throw at us, and it's only at night - when we're alone and our wife or our husband or our school friend is asleep -that we can silently grieve over our own cowardice.
(from *The Devil and Miss Prym* by Paulo Coelho)

Change is the hard thing to do. Making it better is much harder work than watching it die. People will question your motives, tell you that you are wrong. They will say that you can't change the system. It would cause too much upset. They are wrong. It is your church. You promised like me to make it a place worthy of the man who died for us.

It isn't working! There, I've said it again. You don't have to be scared now. You just have to make it better. Start with the promises you made - and see where that takes you.

Section 4:

Being the Church: on the margins

Eleven

OUTSIDE-IN PRIORITIES: UPAS

George Gammack

Rev George Gammack currently works part-time as an Advocacy Worker in mental health in Dundee. Prior to this he was a parish minister in Mastrick in Aberdeen for four years and Whitfield in Dundee for eight years. He is also engaged in mapping church community development work in Scotland for the Churches Community Work Alliance; a "six-month project" which is still going after two years, and George is currently 'trying to write up' an account of what is going on in this area.

The term Priority Area is standard currency both in church and other circles, but the question has to be asked: are Priority Areas really treated as such? This is a question which must be faced by the church, for the truth is that these parishes are often seen as places where ministers get their foot on the bottom rung of the ladder before aspiring to higher things in 'more important places'.

This is not cynicism, but reality. Nor do I say it out of any sense of superiority; for though my credentials are for writing about Urban Priority Area, or UPA, parishes are four years in Mastrick in Aberdeen and eight in Whitifield in Dundee, in neither of these places did I live in the parish, for a number of reasons. My thoughts therefore are also in this sense those of an "outsider"; but also of an insider whose work went on daily in the streets and houses and schools of these peripheral housing schemes.

One thing I learned above all else from this was the great and positive qualities of the people who live in the schemes. The stereotypes of such areas represent them as repositories of crime and vandalism, drugs, family breakdown and all the rest. All these will be found in the UPA, but so will immense volumes of creativity of all kinds - far more, I believe, than is often found in the more prosperous suburbs. In my experience it is the churches in the UPAs which have got closest to giving servant ministry its proper central place, at the same time integrating with it the worship out of which comes the inspiration for new initiatives of creativity.

But are they a priority for the Church? Judged on a reading of *Outside Verdict,* the answer has to be 'no': as on at least one man's journey into the Church of Scotland, they do not rate even a mention. I find this astonishing and really quite inexplicable; however it is a commonly observed phenomenon that many people who have no real involvement in the everyday life and work of the church are those who are most eager to keep it just as it is. The typical 'outsider' has a notoriously conservative angle on the church.

One of the most revelatory statements in *Outside Verdict* is the conclusion in the introduction: 'I, like so many of my fellow countrymen, could not find the Kirk; it was lost. I could find bits of it, good bits, but the Kirk itself seems to have well nigh disappeared' (*Outside Verdict*, p. xxxi). That has echoes of Alice's words as she peered into the looking glass and observed that in the mirror all that was familiar of her present surroundings was to be seen : 'I can see all of it …… *all but the bit behind the fireplace.*' That is the answer to Harry Reid's perplexity. He looked among that which was familiar whereas what he was looking for was hidden. He didn't go into that territory behind the obvious.

It is interesting that the model for the commissioning of *Outside Verdict* was *The Comfortable Pew*, a book similarly commissioned from an outsider, by the Anglican Church in Canada in the sixties. In this book, Pierre Berton - like Harry Reid a journalist – writes on his final page of the need for 'seeing through the murky varnish of wealth, snobbery, self-seeking and apathy which overlays the church, to the essential message at its core'.

The *Outside Verdict* was passed on the mainly visible church. It does not explore beneath the surface and behind the scenes of that institution. And it is of further significance that in the account of a symposium on *Outside Verdict* published in *Theology in Scotland* (Vol.IX, Autumn 2002) there are no voices reported from the housing schemes or the inner city, those places where creative initiatives are very often likely to be found. There is one contribution from an Elder - from the High Kirk of St Giles.

I would like therefore to suggest that we in the church take a fresh look at what is 'the essential message at its core' and to recognise that many of the key signs of this are to be found in places which were not on the itinerary. But thus to consider Priority Areas, and in a sense to turn the 'core view' of the church inside out, is not to be negatively destructive but is about making a positive practical theological affirmation. In stating that what goes on in the Priority Areas is first and foremost what the church should be doing, we are stating our faith in the nature of God who is revealed in the Gospel of Jesus Christ as the creative sharer in the suffering of human kind.

It is my contention that both the greatest suffering and the greatest creativity are to be found in the Priority Areas - mainly urban but also rural. In addition to my parish experience, I have recently travelled throughout the country looking at Church-related Community Work for the Churches Community Work Alliance, and it is my clear perception that it is in the Priority Areas on the whole, that there is the greater vibrancy and responsiveness to the Great Commission: 'Feed my sheep'.

This is the 'divine imperative', the spiritual imperative: 'spiritual' understood not as a "dimension" of life but as a holistic perspective on, and response to, human need. It is loving God and neighbour as self, neither in a purely abstract nor a purely materialistic sense, but as the recognition of whatever is lacking in the food and music of life, and taking steps to remedy it. Spirituality is about sacramental wholeness, affording each and all a sense of self as valued in the great and beautiful order of creation. It is in the search for such a practical theology that transcends the brokenness of life, that I believe the best evidence is to be found in the places of greatest adversity.

The 'essential message at its core' therefore is clearly stated for the church:

> I was hungry and you fed me, thirsty and you gave me a drink; I was a
> stranger and you received me in your homes, naked and you clothed me; I
> was sick and you took care of me, in prison and you visited me.
>
> (Matthew 25:35)

And so I'll follow this with some indicators - in the form of the 'seven churches' listed below - of where and how we should be looking, working, and building

1. The Church for the Hungry

'When the roll is called up yonder...' The words of the old hymn are given a new slant by those places where the Kirk is recognising and meeting people's basic needs to be fed. One minister responded to the work of a local church café in a UPA by saying, 'The church is not just about bacon rolls'. Yes; and the sacrament of Holy Communion is not just about bread and wine, but about a fullness of life, of which material sustenance is a primary dimension. Priority Areas are places where the church is meeting and responding to people in accessible locations, where, in the sharing of bacon rolls, they may together touch and handle things unseen.

Thus if he had got up very early one morning and made his way up to Dundee, Harry Reid might have called in at my old stamping-ground in Whitfield, where he could have had cornflakes with the school-kids, and stayed on to have tea and toast, and lunch too, with the older folk at the Day Centre.

2. The Church for the Stranger

The author of *Outside Verdict* did not apparently visit any of those places where the needs of refugees and asylum seekers are being responded to, where the basics of clothing and friendship are being extended to those who find themselves in exile in a foreign land. Such is one of the highest and holiest forms of service. As the writer of Hebrews puts it, 'do not neglect to show hospitality to strangers, for by doing that some have entertained angels without knowing it' (Hebrews 13:2).

3. The Church for the Prisoner

The following verse in Hebrews then tells us: 'Remember those who are in prison, as though you were in prison with them; those who are being tortured, as though you yourselves were being tortured' (Hebrews 13.3). In this context, it's an interesting coincidence that the prime mover in the commissioning of *Outside Verdict* has now taken up a post as HM Inspector of Prisons in Scotland, and is urging churches to be more involved in integrating ex-prisoners into a sense of belonging and community. Are we up to it?

4. The Church for the Homeless

Relegated to the last four pages of *Outside Verdict* - but at least it's there – are the topics of soup and sleep for homeless people: but why is there no visit to, or mention of, the Scottish Churches Housing Agency for example, or the Glasgow Lodging House Mission? Where, in the this book's portrayal of the great sweep of organised religion in Scotland, is the divine mission to those at the utter bottom of it all?

By this I mean, not just those who are in the streets, but those who are homeless in other ways – for instance, those who have spent long years in institutions to do with mental illness and learning disability. For example, for *Outside Verdict*, the Church in Aberdeen is Beechgrove, and its celebrity pulpit. If the author didn't find anything else, it was again because he was looking in the wrong places, and only for the kind of church of days gone by that he wanted to find. If he had gone a couple of miles across the city he would have found - for those who know where to look - a number of flats which form a local church project for people with learning disabilities, providing them with 'an ordinary life' as far as possible. A new meaning to the concept of 'house church'.

5. The Church for Creativity

Beauty for Brokenness - the apt and moving title of a song by Graham Kendrick. The initiative of creative artistry in word and image, in dramatic presentation, as exemplified by the Netherbow, is acknowledged in *Outside Verdict*, but perceived as something to be developed in the big posh places; whereas, for example, a visit to 'The Village' at St James's Pollok - where part of that great edifice has been transformed into the 'Local

Village', the 'Bible Village' and the 'Global Village' - would have given a wholly different perspective on what can be achieved in a local setting. As Donald Smith puts it so well in *Art of the Parish*, 'If it is not grounded in Aberdeen, Harare, Auchtermuchty and Bethlehem, then it is simply not real...all truly worthwhile art reaches the universal by working with the immediate reality of place, people and material. Otherwise it lacks authenticity'. Thus we cannot talk of the Kirk having 'undersold itself as a patron of the arts' or of art being 'harnessed for the greater good of the Kirk' without the cultivation at ground level of the imaginative capacity. We need to learn lessons of theological imagination, the Gospel for today, to counter the paralysis of dreary dogmatic fixations.

And it's not just 'drawin 'n paintin'. It is about being active in the whole world of creation. If we travel out from Glasgow City Centre in a north-easterly direction, we come across two recently constructed parks, one in the grounds of a church and the other at the source of the Molendinar Burn. These are local projects, not nominally or explicitly 'church' - but then neither was Jeremiah's field. Many 'secular' places are crying out for 'spiritual' transformation.

6. The Church in the Secular Temple

Remaining in the East End of Glasgow there is the magnificent Bambury Regeneration Centre. Not a 'church building', but a place offering all round facilities for body, mind and soul. Within the building, among the bacon rolls (what again?), music, computers, football, youth project, arts and Crafts is PEEK, or Possibilities for East End Kids - for which the posh name is 'the Gallowgate and Calton Children's Project' - run by Glasgow Inner East End Churches Together. It has no religious trappings, this church – it's incognito in the secular temple.

Likewise the Eric Liddell Centre, within a more patently 'holy' edifice in the rather different surroundings of Morningside: a multiplex temple of prison-like landings reaching up to heaven. Or a much-longer standing example of the Lanthorn in Livingston, where church inhabits community centre and, in some of the caring work that goes on, old and reassuring boundaries of sacred and secular are challengingly dissolved.

This raises the question of ownership. The blurring of identities is in this respect an asset. It opens up possibilities for community ownership, community being defined not primarily in geographical terms but by the quality of relatedness among the people for whom the provision exists. In this the church as conventionally understood may indeed lose itself. But is not that the way in which we are advised it may find itself?

7. The Church at Work

I can find no reference in *Outside Verdict* to the Scottish Churches Industrial Mission, which I must say, I consider a very questionable omission. Through this agency the tentacles of the church reach into all sorts of places, from those giant citadels of consumerism such as the Braehead Shopping Centre in Renfrew, through factories and offices, to the fields of sorrow where there is pain in the heart of the farming community.

These 'seven churches' represent areas of work that should be seen as 'central' rather than 'peripheral' church. The church is involved in these areas (which Reid somewhat disparagingly refers to as 'practical evidence of utilitarian assistance'), but it is seen as secondary to pulpit, pew and psalm. Without abandoning the latter, the task for the church is to shift the above spheres of work into the centre also. This means adopting as its priority *organising itself for caring*, not by way of an authoritarian centralised bureaucracy, but by concerted initiatives, locally built and run, imaginatively engaging the assets of people and place to form the living, contemporary Body of Christ.

It all hinges on what is our understanding of 'faith' and 'religion'. If these are identified wholly with services of worship (the 'real church') then we need a major readjustment in our thinking; not to replace this with 'empty social activism', but to make the servant ministry to the dispossessed as central and 'real church' as hymns and prayers. The division between these two dimensions has to be recognised as being untenable. The total identification of church with worship is out of balance, and contrary to the Biblical pattern in which the excesses to which this can lead are on many occasions given short shrift. Piety practised in a vacuum too easily becomes an empty and offensive ritual, as with the perversion of the practice of fasting denounced through God's prophet:

> The kind of fasting I want is this: remove the chains of oppression and the yoke of injustice and let the oppressed go free. Share your food with the hungry and open your homes to the homeless poor. Give clothes to those who have nothing to wear, and do not refuse to help your own relatives.
> Then my favour will shine on you like the morning sun, and your wounds will be quickly healed. I will always be with you to save you; my presence will protect you on every side. (Isaiah 58:6-8)

James Sweeney, in 'From Story to Policy', reminds us of how faith communities are now in favour with government, as partners in countering social exclusion. They may be publicly funded, he says, but adds: 'financial support of religious organisations is restricted to the non-religious activities, i.e. providing meals, a night shelter, counselling services etc.'[1]

Here is the crux of the matter: the perception of these things as non-religious, as opposed to the "real religion" of the Sunday morning sanctuary. This is the barrier that has to be overcome: that religion perhaps can never be distilled in any pure form out of the everyday momentum of life, and an over-concentration on temple worship can lead us into neglecting all those prophetic warnings on this subject. What Sweeney calls 'faith-based social action' is not a mere supporting act for a full-blast rendering of 'Onward Christian Soldiers', and a pious muttering of 'Our Father'. It is the real thing. As he points out, we are not dealing with 'a proselytising form of faith, not even, one might say, a highly "religious" kind of faith, but rather a type of faith which keeps close to the human struggle to assert the value of humanity, and a faith that seeks expression in service'.

The Gospels are undergirded by love expressed as caring, the engagement with physical and mental disorder, story-telling and feeding. Why is it hard for mainline organised religion to come to terms with this, rather than be centred - as it is - on verbal proclamation? There is no contradiction between the two other than that which the church artificially, and often neurotically, creates. The balance is there in the Gospels, the primacy of care for people, the actual form of expression a straight-forward human one, in the enactment of which transcendence breaks forth and speaks for itself.

In my experience, it is the churches in the UPAs which have got closest to giving servant ministry its proper central place, at the same time integrated with the worship out of which comes the inspiration for new initiatives of creativity.

This is backed up by comments in the UPA report to the 2002 Assembly: for instance that the UPA congregations 'seemed more alive than those in more affluent communities',[2] and the highlighted summary statement in the report identifies the core issue with uncompromising sharpness:

> The whole church must recognise that to be committed to the poorest and most vulnerable is the gospel imperative facing us all, not just the churches in the urban priority areas.

It is because of its failure to begin to acknowledge this 'gospel imperative' that I am so unhappy about *Outside Verdict*: its sad neglect, not just of the existence of the churches in the UPAs, but of all the creative, cross-boundary initiatives which are again well-documented in the above report (e.g. 2.2.9.4), renders *Outside Verdict* an exercise in making that bit richer the 'resource-rich church' and further impoverishing, if not abandoning the 'resource-poor' church referred to in that report.

[1] *From Story to Policy: Social Inclusion, Empowerment and the Churches* by James Sweeney, with Denise Hannah and Kevin McMahon (2001), Von Hugel Institute, St Edmund's College, University of Cambridge.

[2] *Report to the General Assembly* (2002), Board of National Mission. *Reports to the General Assembly 2002*, The Church of Scotland Board of Practice and Procedure.

Thus the feeding and housing and caring church, which can also tell meaningful stories both in private and in public, is the true church of the Good News which should be embraced by all. Here is the opportunity for comprehensive cross-boundary working, including the need for 'evangelicals' not to split off from the rest of the church on the ideological grounds of differences in scriptural interpretation, but to form partnerships to work together in the front line of real evangelical caring - with no salvation strings attached.

This demands a radical shift in practical perspective from all concerned. A major redeployment of the church's energies and facilities from jumble sale domesticity into really strong local initiatives for the least and the lost in our world; and a reappraisal of, for instance, the 'evangelical' priorities which has Andrew McGowan place 'a Church that cares' sixth and last in his manifesto list (*Life and Work* August 2002). It is not divisions we need: 'There is no longer Jew or Greek, there is no longer slave or free, there is no longer male and female; for all of you are one in Christ Jesus' (Galatians 3:28). How about that for a manifesto?

The unconditional love to which Paul movingly refers is not an also-ran coming in some way after the front-runners of doctrine and dogma. It is that which can bring all together to abandon their labels, prejudices and presuppositions and work together. The *Church without Walls* report therapeutically reminds us that 'the church's continued existence by grace alone... challenges us to do as the Jews did in Exile, to rebuild God-honouring community, in an alien environment, but to do it non-anxiously.'[3] Such is the servant church, the Church for others.

Thus also, to make partnerships and alliances with anyone else who also cares enough to do the work of feeding and healing and housing people and creating beautiful places out of broken spaces. We can find that in parts, good parts, but that is not enough.Connecting up to the focal areas of human need requires to be a priority, everywhere.

This will not be resolved by foraging around to find 'An Old Kirk in New Scotland'. Top-down programmes and pronouncements, theoretical theology and big events are not what is needed. The cross stands outside the gate of these things, wrecked life symbolised by the wrecked car outside the bounds of the city. So maybe it is not possible. Maybe the work of re-creation will always have to go on off-centre, be literally a wee bit eccentric and be seen as that, if it is seen at all, by the main 'body of believers'. As long as the latter realise that such extra-mural servant ministry requires more, and not less, faith, and that the new resurrection life which follows may rise in unpredictable ways in unexpected places. It has always been so.

---

[3] Report of the Special Commission Anent Review and Reform; *Reports to the General Assembly of the Church of Scotland 2001*, reprinted as *Church without Walls, Parish Education Publications 2001*

ON OTHER PEOPLE'S TERRITORY: CHAPLAINCY

Alison Elliot

Alison Elliot is Associate Director of Edinburgh University's Centre for Theology and Public Issues. She does a great deal of ecumenical work nationally and internationally, and is Convener of the Scottish Churches Forum of ACTS.

If you're looking for signs of the church, the obvious place to start is in church buildings or offices. But a lot of the church's work is done on other people's territory. And the area of ministry that exemplifies this best is that of chaplaincy.

Chaplains come in all shapes and sizes. Most people will have come across a chaplain in school or in hospital. They also serve in universities, in prisons and in the armed forces. Recently, industrial chaplains have moved into airports and shopping malls, as well as continuing their more traditional role in factories and offices. The demand for chaplains is growing. At the same time, the context in which they are operating is changing rapidly, and so their role is being continually reassessed. This makes it an interesting area in which to ask fundamental questions about the church and its mission.

Chaplains at work

Chaplains find themselves doing a whole range of things:

- In a prison, a chaplain shares a cup of coffee with some prisoners – special "civvy" coffee, unlike what's usually provided for them.

- In the mess, a chaplain listens in on a conversation about the morality of warfare, all the more intense as the servicemen face up to their own mortality in the context of hardship, fear and of making the ultimate sacrifice.

- A hospital midwife is given support by her chaplain, after a mother she'd got to know well during her first pregnancy loses her second baby.

- A primary head teacher discusses with the school chaplain the programme for the term's assemblies.

- The chaplain to the local authority develops a liturgy of baptism to be used in the home of an employee with no church connection, who wants to mark the baby's birth appropriately.

- On a university Research Ethics Committee, the chaplain takes her seat.

Beyond that, there are tasks chaplains undertake in all the contexts in which they work. They often help an institution to shape moments of celebration, such as graduations, or the kirking of the council. But they also have to cope with moments of tragedy, such as helping the bereaved at the time of a death, helping a community deal with something like the foot-and-mouth crisis, or ministering to an institution in shock after a young suicide.

In Chaucer's *Canterbury Tales,* the chaplain was on a pilgrimage along with other people and was the carrier of sacred things. Chaplains frequently talk about journeying alongside people, and being on hand to share with them the comforts and insights of faith. They often say that what they do is 'loiter with intent'. In order to be of use to people when they need them, they have to establish a presence in the host institution, to become an approachable 'weel-kent face'. The loitering pays dividends when someone finds they can turn to their chaplain in stormy times.

It begs the question, however, of what the "intent" is. Proselytising is out, and the balance between helping someone and exploiting their weakness has to be strictly observed. But there are other things chaplains can offer. They set out to link people into community, away from the individualising forces in society. They listen to the stories of life and tell the stories of faith. In this way, they add quality to the life of individuals and of institutions.

The context of chaplaincy

Chaplains meet people in very specific places, which are designed for very particular purposes – working, healing, teaching, containing prisoners, preparing to fight a war, maintaining law and order. On the face of it, they meet only a part of a person; yet in all cases it is a significant part of them, and one which provides a valuable entry point into the rest of their experience.

The vast majority of the people they meet are unchurched. Some will know nothing about religion and care even less. Some will have separated from any religious upbringing they once had. Some may be violently antagonistic to any institutionalised religion because of the deep hurt they have experienced at its hand. Some will be committed people of faith.

Chaplains cannot assume that a person's faith experience matches theirs. They may be Jewish, Muslim, Hindu - and chaplaincies are increasingly inter-faith in the service they offer. They are certainly ecumenical in their outreach, and frequently explicitly ecumenical in the structure of the chaplaincy team. This freeing of the chaplaincy service from its Christian, or even denominational, roots can sometimes cause misunderstanding and hurt to those who see the chaplain as a representative in the institution of their denomination. However, the chaplains themselves, sensitive to the spiritual needs of people from their own religious tradition, are generally anxious to be in a position to extend that care appropriately to others.

Many of the people that chaplains come across are young – in school, university, armed forces and so on - and do not have the experience of worship or church culture, even though they are open to finding out. It's very easy to stifle that interest, with church practices that are scary and alienating. Yet another group needs the comfort zone of the religious tradition that's familiar to them when they're going through a stressful time. Chaplains need to find ways of reaching out to both groups.

The fact that the demand for chaplaincy is growing, however, probably reflects another trend in society. Increasingly, people are willing to express an interest in spirituality; and institutions recognise that, whatever may be happening to rates of church membership, members of their community do have spiritual needs that should be addressed. One Vice-Chancellor referred to the chaplaincy as the hub of the community or, switching metaphors, a lightning conductor into the hotbed of emotion and commitment of young people. There's a need out there that chaplains are able to address.

Going native?

It can take a lot of negotiating and persuading to set up a new chaplaincy in an institution but, once there, chaplains are generally treated as honoured guests. Their role cuts across the hierarchies and fiefdoms of the place and in principle they have access to people at all levels.

But being a guest in an institution like a shipyard or a hospital can sometimes be an uncomfortable experience. Guests are expected to behave themselves, to conform to the social rules of their host, to be part of a particular culture. The danger of chaplains being compromised by these expectations is, in principle, always present. Moreover, their Christian calling to stand beside the vulnerable has the potential to bring them into conflict with the powers that be. Of course, this is the reality for all followers of Christ, but for the chaplain it may be a calling that puts them on the spot in a particularly public way.

By and large, host institutions do not see it in this way. Rather, they consider the chaplain to be somebody who helps the institution be what it should be. In the army, it's important to build teamwork, to build respect for other people and to encourage particular spiritual values. The chaplain is seen as a natural ally in this task. Universities want to look after the social, cultural and intellectual development of their students, not just to deliver graduates on time and within budget. The chaplaincy is often a key player in offering their students a more rounded education. A hospital's commitment to health and healing sits easily alongside a commitment to spiritual well-being and, indeed, the World Health Organisation has added a reference to spirituality to its definition of what health is. Yet in the busyness of a modern hospital, and in the tough financial environment of today's NHS, it is easy to lose sight of these central purposes. Hospital chaplains not only contribute to a patient's well-being by paying attention to their spiritual needs but they can also help to create an ethos in which nurses and doctors are freed from a target-reaching mentality to be the healers that they came into medicine to be.

Particular institutions can point to the economic advantage of having a well-resourced chaplaincy. Increasingly, there is evidence for hospitals that, if you deliver the rounded care that is needed - and that includes spiritual care - hospital staff are happier, burnout is less and the health outcomes are better. Universities are also keen to hold on to their students, and enriching the student experience through the support and stimulation that chaplaincy can provide is money well spent. Value for money should not be a central motivation for the provision of chaplaincy, but it does no harm to point to its real benefits in contributing to a thriving community.

Chaplains stand Janus-like between the institution they minister to and the church. Understanding the host institution is an important part of their job. From the inside, they will probably discover that the public face hides a much more complex reality. The simple narrative of the institution will be known but does not necessarily determine the attitudes and motivations of people within it. On the face of it, having empathy with a company whose principal purpose is to make profits or with military units whose mottoes are 'Prepare for war' or 'Attack and protect' may appear to be hopelessly compromising. Yet it is precisely there that a well-informed and trusted minister of the Gospel can be of particular value in unravelling the complex conflicts that society of any age throws at us.

Ministers and chaplains

'I hope you'll get a real job soon!' Chaplains often report that they are made to feel second-best ministers - and well-meaning comments like this don't help!

Chaplains frequently express their relief at being away from parish ministry, if that has been part of their earlier experience. They're glad to be released from fabric concerns and the burden of a building, although chaplains in traditional sectors can sometimes find that they are heirs to a chapel that is just as constraining as a church.

They tend to enjoy the freedom that comes from being distant from the concerns and expectations of institutionalised religion. They meet people in the context of significant moments in their lives, and most chaplains find this refreshing compared with an increasingly artificial congregational community. Some may find the isolation of their role difficult to cope with, while others launch themselves into networks of support within their new community.

Parish ministry, of course, is changing. Chaplains may be right in thinking that, at a congregational level, churches have backed themselves into their buildings. However, beckoning the church out into the local community is precisely what the *Church without Walls* Report was trying to do. And once outside the walls, the minister who takes seriously ministry to the whole parish will find the same mix of attitudes and faith backgrounds that chaplains often find stimulating as well as frustrating within their context. So the distinctions between parish ministry and chaplaincy are perhaps not as great as they seem to be.

The task of the church does not begin and end within the boundaries of the chaplain's institution. Continuing the care of someone who has been in hospital or in prison or in the armed forces calls for liaison, not just with a local parish minister but with other bodies, possibly church-run, possibly not, that develop a special sensitivity to their needs. And, before anyone ends up in hospital or in prison, it may be that their social circumstances have helped to put them there. The complex interaction between poverty and both ill-health and crime means that the chaplain should not lose touch with the work that churches and other organisations do in the fight against poverty. All of these are forms of ministry, and it would make sense to enable people to move freely between them, rather than entrenching a distinction between parish ministry and chaplaincy.

However, amongst these forms of ministry, chaplains often have particularly well-honed insights and rich experiences. People in the rest of the church and the wider community should hear more from them. All ministers have to walk with people facing death, but hospice chaplains do it daily; and prison chaplains must have reflected more than most on matters of guilt and forgiveness. They are the church's experts.

Chaplains have colleagues who are highly trained professionals in their own disciplines. The question of how far chaplaincy itself should be professionalised is a lively one. In Scotland, healthcare chaplaincy is leading the way with the appointment through the Scottish Executive of a Healthcare Chaplaincy Training and Development Officer along with a seconded colleague. Masters degrees in healthcare chaplaincy and in military chaplaincy are either up and running, or in the pipeline. At the same time, much of the value of chaplaincy is its spontaneity and its lack of institutionalisation. In some of the newer areas of chaplaincy, the chaplain is a real pioneer, doing truly original work. Having a professional qualification is not the same as doing a professional job and there may be other ways of providing support, ensuring accountability and continuing professional development.

'If this is the margin, where's the centre?'

On the margins, or at the heart of people's lives? On the fringes of the church, or at the frontier of mission? Second-class ministers - or the church of the future?

The growth in chaplaincy is part of a response to the forms of community and identity that we have nowadays. Where we live is only a small part of who we are. At times, our patterns of church life seem to be responding to ways of living that probably disappeared from most of Scotland two hundred years ago. There may well be value – indeed there is – in the church cutting across communities of interest to give support to communities of place. But if we mean what we say about there being no no-go areas for the Gospel, then we have to take seriously the challenge of engaging with the lives people lead most of the time on their own terms. And that's where chaplaincy comes in.

But it's not just a case of going with the flow. Airports are bustling places where lots of people congregate. But they are also places of parting and of crisis and it's because of this human need that there's a place for a chaplain. People are leaving farming, yet that's precisely why the church needs to be alongside that community in transition to share its pain and to develop an informed Christian perspective on this crisis. And new needs arise all the time. Community mental health chaplaincy is now needed as more people with mental health problems are cared for in the community rather than in hospital.

If the church is to be made up of 'fishers of men', it has to risk getting its feet wet! As it shapes a ministry for the kaleidoscope of the twentieth century, it can learn a lot from the experience of its chaplains.

BEING THE CHURCH: AN AERIAL VIEW

John Miller

Very Rev Dr John D Miller *has been minister of the parish of Castlemilk East since 1971. He was Convener of the Urban Priority Areas Subcommittee of the Mission and Evangelism Resources Committee of the Board of National Mission for four years. John was Moderator of the General Assembly of the Church of Scotland in 2001/2.*

Leadership in the Church of Scotland

One morning early in May 2002 (the year in which I served as Moderator of the General Assembly) as I entered the Church Offices at 121 George Street I discovered I had once more forgotten my security pass. The steward at the desk said, 'Again? You'll get your books! You've got till the end of the month.' And of course, he was quite right - because at the end of the month I would cease to be Moderator and would never be back in the premises in that role again.

Few institutions change their chief figurehead every year. The Church of Scotland has done so religiously for the last 400 years. I've heard the system called 'the embodiment of distrust', and in truth the Scottish character has shown a reluctance to entrust authority to any individual for a long period. During my year in office I recognised that while this annual replacement of the senior figure eliminates the danger of dictatorship, it leaves a vacuum of leadership in the structure of the institution. Where, then, does leadership lie in the Church of Scotland? At this critical moment who will lead the Kirk in formulating and implementing its response to its problems?

A panorama of the Church

The Moderator is popularly thought of as the leader of the Church of Scotland. For one year in office, the Moderator will attend to a variety of duties on behalf of the Church as a whole. But the Moderator's only executive function is to chair the General Assembly, which meets for one week of the year. The Assembly is the Kirk's only Chief Executive. The Convener of the Kirk's highest spending committee is answerable finally to no-one but the Assembly.

I experienced a great contrast between my role as a parish minister in a Glasgow housing scheme and my role as Moderator of the General Assembly. Stepping from the pavements of Castlemilk to the corridors of power in one swift movement, I attained a vantage point from which to view the nation-wide Church of Scotland, and also to encounter its reputation overseas.

Each Moderator visits five Presbyteries, the Church of Scotland's administrative areas. In 2001-2002 the Moderator's visits included three rural Presbyteries: Sutherland in the far north of Scotland, Abernethy on Speyside, and the area round Oban called Lorn and Mull. The others were Irvine and Kilmarnock in the West, and Edinburgh in the East. In addition to visiting many individual congregations in the course of the year, often to celebrate a major anniversary or a successful programme of renewal, I chose to visit seven housing schemes or inner-city areas. Because of the major role played by the Kirk over the centuries, the Moderator has access to discussion with the leaders of local community life and with many people who help to shape Scotland, giving an unparalleled opportunity to assess the current place of the Church in local and national life.

One astonishing feature of the Church of Scotland, as Harry Reid notes in his review of its worship, is its enormous diversity. Within the one institution are to be found city congregations of five hundred worshippers, composed of well-to-do men and women of professional standing, and congregations of 15 or 20 people characterised by gatherings in small churches in Highland glens. There are congregations who have met each week in the same historic building for centuries, marking the passage of time by their continuous witness, and there are heroic meetings of the faithful in transitional premises in city housing areas quite recently founded but already undergoing the trials of social regeneration. Equally in evidence is a wide spectrum of theological outlook. There are still congregations where no woman may be an elder and no woman would be considered appropriate for the pulpit, and others where women are encouraged and relied upon in both roles. There are congregations where a strict view on infant baptism sees very few babies baptised, and others where no child is ever refused baptism. There are congregations where wine and cheese parties are part of the social life, and others where only tea will be on offer, some where the spiritual focus is on profound individual quest, and others where the congregation is communally engaged in major social action.

During the year as Moderator, I had the opportunity to witness life in a wide variety of parishes, and to ask whether there are common threads which run throughout the Church of Scotland and constitute it as a single institution. Throughout the year I was also asking myself about the place of the Church in our increasingly secular society.

Not death but change

I saw a Church undergoing immense changes, a Church in transition from one role to another. I did not see a Church that was dying.

I think particularly of a visit to Nigeria where I had the opportunity to meet the President of the Federal Republic. He expressed his gratitude to Scotland and to the Scots who had brought the Gospel to Nigeria 150 years before. This, he said, was 'a gift beyond price'. He went on to speak of other things which the Church had brought. The Scots in general had brought universal, high-quality education, and a tradition of integrity in public life. Presbyterianism in particular, he said, by engaging lay people as well as ordained ministers in the government of the Church, had prepared people for participatory democracy. He spoke of his country's 'eternal gratitude' to Scotland for these gifts and hoped that I would bring those expressions of gratitude back home.

Lasting value in an age of change

In these categories of gratitude, the Nigerian President expressed issues which the Church still addresses in a way from which society can benefit. Although the Church's role is changing, it can perform an extremely important function still for society.

He referred first to the Gospel. In a fragmented era, this post-modernist time with so many different forms and sets of values available to people, the Church's perspective on life is, to use a modern phrase, holistic. It is one of the more complete, holistic systems available to people today. For within the circle of faith, the whole of life - indeed the whole of the *universe* - is embraced.

In earlier generations there was, as it were, an incoming tide upon which people were carried into the Church and the tide of faith was at the full for many generations. But the tide has been ebbing for decades and has left many people without any contact with the Gospel and its holistic view of the world and of individual life. But the Church has a message which through 2000 years has been proved able to transform people's lives, and give purpose and encouragement to their best hopes.

The tide of faith seems to be on the move, coming in again. More and more people are expressing an interest in issues of faith. Many, however, are not finding their questions addressed within the Church's own structures, and the Church will have to find a way to reach people beyond its walls and express to them the perspectives which have enriched previous generations.

Education, social care, rites of passage.

At the time of the Reformation, it was John Knox's vision that in every parish there would be a church and a school, and from that time Scotland had a tradition of high quality education made available to everyone. The Church has always had at its centre the sense that, for people to develop fully their personality and fulfil their destiny as human beings, they require to be offered high quality education. In 1872, the Church transferred its responsibility for education to the state, and since then the state has done its utmost to fulfil that vision of an educated population. But there remains an inequality in the provision. The children who come from areas of disadvantage need the greatest assistance in obtaining a good education but often receive the least. The Church has always maintained an interest in the education of all, and that will continue to be a major concern for the faith communities.

Care for the most vulnerable has been at the heart of the Christian faith - the 'works of mercy' as they have often been called. These include the care of people who are ill and those who are elderly and frail and unable to look after themselves, the care of children in trouble and of people in prison. Many of these areas of social life have now become responsibilities of the state, with local or central authorities both funding and providing the services. But the Church's special interest remains, and from within it there will continue to be a voice focusing on these vital areas of human existence.

There are other aspects of human existence, the 'rites of passage' - birth, marriage and death - on which the Church has its own particular perspective, with a language still full of meaning even for people whose contact with the Church may have been minimal.

Public and private morality

For centuries the Church acted as an arbiter of private and public morality. The Nigerian President paid tribute to the Scottish tradition of integrity in public life, recognising how important it was that people who carried responsibility for decision-making and for implementing policy in public life had been trained in moral behaviour. The tradition of unselfishness which lies within much Christian teaching was the hallmark of a great deal of public life in Scotland through the centuries.

This remains one of the aims of any society - that its public servants should be utterly trustworthy. From the cradle of the faith of the Church comes encouragement and substance for people's public moral life. But as the years have gone on, questions of private and public morality have come under great scrutiny, and the role of the Church in prescribing how people might live has been diminished, and indeed set aside by many people. Yet the issues of morality - how people behave, how families are to be sustained, how children are to be brought up - these remain key questions for our society. The Church's experience in discussing and formulating thinking on these matters will continue to have significance.

It has often been noted that people take an interest in 'soap operas ' and programmes like 'Big Brother' in order to see how other people deal with huge issues, looking as it were for moral guidance from the patterns of behaviour exhibited by other people. This is an important new way for people to receive ideas about how to live themselves. But from within the Church comes that particular form of morality which submits itself not simply to public scrutiny, but is accountable to God. This perspective will continue to appeal to many people to whom the relative answers given by other forms of moral thinking prove inadequate. After global poverty, one of the greatest public issues is nuclear power. The Church has a developed tradition on the issues of morality in relation to war and terror. It will continue to contribute significantly to the discussions about how to attain multinational nuclear disarmament.

Sin, decay, and death

But it is in relation to life and death, particularly the issue of death, that the Church's vocabulary reaches beyond what can be embraced by politics, economics or sociology alone. Even if the date of 11th September 2001 does not mark, as many have thought, a major turning-point in the history of the world, the elemental question of death and its meaning continues to address our society. The gathered community of people of faith has important reflections to offer. If there was no congregation, no gathering of people of faith, then the perspective of faith would be absent from community life. Christian faith confronts sin, decay and death, those elements in human life which wear hope away. Each generation has to articulate the faith for itself. In the climate of our current culture this is no easy task. But the church can offer these reflections to the entire local community. The church is made up of congregations. The congregation is the church's contribution to community life.

Central and local

Harry Reid's book *Outside Verdict* has a tendency to reflect on the administrative structures of the church as if they were themselves the church. The overwhelming thrust of his Twenty-One Proposals for renewing and reviving the Kirk is towards the central structures. My own prolonged local experience in a small, though densely-populated, urban parish, together with the panoramic view to which I had such privileged access for the year as Moderator, both confirm in me a conviction. In the Presbyterian Church, the congregations are the leaders. It is the local church, the congregation, which will guarantee a future for Christianity as a vital part of our culture.

No local congregation can accomplish this task, however, if it is isolated from the rest of the Church. It is the task of the central structures to secure the unity of the Church and the stability of the shared enterprise.

The two essential ingredients: Ministry and buildings

The priorities of the central institution, therefore, must be to ensure the supply of these two essential constituent elements of congregational life: the trained Ordained and Lay Ministry and the local church building.

Ministry:

The forecast reduction in the number of ordained ministers has alarmed all who have recognised the importance of the trained Ministry. The compilers of the 1560 *Book of Discipline* were in no doubt that well-trained ministers were the key to the future quality of church life. They instituted rigorous tests and examinations for their selection:

> We are not ignorant that the rarity of godly and learned men shall seem to
> some a just reason why so strait and sharp examination would not be taken
> universally, because it shall appear that the most part of the kirks shall have
> no minister at all. But let these men understand that the lack of able men shall
> not excuse us before God if, by our consent, unable men be placed over the
> flock of Christ Jesus. ...[1]

They recognised that in a time of shortage of ordained ministers there was a vital role for lay leaders:

> For Readers: To the kirks where no ministers can be had presently must be
> appointed the most apt men that distinctly can read the Common Prayers and
> the Scriptures, till they grow to greater perfection; and in the process of time
> he that is but a reader may attain to the further degree, and by consent of the
> Kirk and discreet ministers, may be permitted to administer the Sacraments....
> (IV. Concerning Ministers and Their Lawful Election.[2])

[1] 1560 *Book of Discipline: The History of the Reformation of Religion in Scotland*, by John Knox; Andrew Melrose, London 1905.

[2] The compilers of the *Book of Discipline* foresaw, moreover, that a shortage of ministers would present difficulties for conducting all the funerals. Already facing this problem in our present generation, the Kirk today has not adopted the solution suggested by the *Book of Discipline*:
"To avoid all inconveniences, we judge it best that there be neither singing nor reading at the burial. ... Either shall the ministers for the most part be occupied in preaching funeral sermons or else they shall have respect to persons, preaching at the burial of the rich and honourable, but keeping silence when the poor or despised departeth; and this the ministers cannot do with safe conscience."
1560 *Book of Discipline*: XIV Of Burial.

While, therefore, we may be entering a time of shortage of ordained ministers, we are already developing alternative patterns of local leadership, as an earlier generation was required to do before us. It is alarming, however, that at a time when we anticipate a shortage of ordained ministers, and the role of lay leadership is likely to be of particular importance, the Kirk's Board of National Mission has suspended the recruitment and training of Deacons, and the lack of sustained funding has led to the closure of the Scottish Churches' Open College.

Buildings:

The Kirk's buildings, many of them undoubtedly part of Scotland's architectural glory, have the potential to endanger the Kirk's central role of addressing the Gospel to people in today's culture. Local congregations are under constant pressure to siphon energy and finance towards the care and maintenance of their buildings. The Kirk will have to ensure that its local congregations have only such buildings as they can sustain without distorting this central role. We have something to learn from Local Authorities who have replaced their entire Secondary School building stock with standard-design premises. The economies of scale combined with the accurately-calculable maintenance costs will liberate funds and energy for the programme for living which takes place within the buildings.

Leadership in the Church Without Walls

In the office of Moderator, the Church of Scotland has a tool which can perform a vital service for the Church in maintaining the focus on its vital central functions. The Moderator can articulate the major themes for the whole Church. In this media-orientated age, the task could be performed more effectively if the Moderator held office for a longer period, perhaps for three years, as is the case in a number of other Presbyterian Churches.

The *Church without Walls Report*[3] has encapsulated exactly the right focus for today's Church. Leadership of the Church will be exercised at local level through the congregation. But this will be accomplished only if the congregation moves beyond its walls, into the life of the local community. Then the challenge and power of the Christian Gospel will again be accessible to the population of Scotland.

---

[3] Report of the Special Commission Anent Review and Reform; *Reports to the General Assembly of the Church of Scotland 2001*, reprinted as *Church without Walls*, Parish Education Publications 2001.